A TRIBUTE

She was loved and trusted by every man who ever knew her.

To the eyes of the young men who looked upon her with warmth and affection she had beauty unsurpassed.

To her friends she was gentle, stanch, loyal and a protectoress; to her enemies she was a lightning bolt from the skies, a ruthless and total destroyer.

An inanimate piece of machinery, a mass of tubes, wire, steel, aluminum, she flew like an angel.

She was the Hawker Hurricane.

THE HURRICANE STORY

Paul Gallico

A BERKLEY MEDALLION BOOK
published by
BERKLEY PUBLISHING CORP.

To those who designed, built, tested,
repaired, modified, flew and loved
the HURRICANE.

COPYRIGHT © 1959, BY PAUL GALLICO

Published by arrangement with
Doubleday & Company, Inc.

BERKLEY MEDALLION BOOKS are published by
Berkley Publishing Corporation,
15 East 26th Street, New York 10, New York

Printed in the United States of America

PART ONE

SHE WAS LOVED and trusted by every man who ever knew her.

To the eyes of the young men who looked upon her with warmth and affection she had beauty unsurpassed.

To her friends she was gentle, stanch, loyal and a protectoress; to her enemies she was a lightning bolt from the skies, a ruthless and total destroyer.

She was unique in the heavens, for there was nothing she could not do there when called upon by those who loved and needed her.

An inanimate piece of machinery, a mass of tubes, wire, steel, aluminum, she flew like an angel.

She had no vices.

In the hands of the young men who mastered her and became her lovers she saved England and all that rest of the world that cherished the right of freedom.

She was the Hawker Hurricane.

There will never be a time when the story of the Battle of Britain, that struggle where the thousand and one exploits of the defenders—the few against the many—merged into one gigantic symphony of fighting fury, gallantry and human perseverance in the face of odds, will not be told and retold. But in this struggle on which the fate of the world hinged, another element was added to that thin margin that separates victory from defeat in war. That element was a flying machine.

There had been fighter aircraft before this, in the First World War, when men in flimsy kites had dueled in the sky like ancient knights. However, in those days the fate of the nations for whom they fought was not dependent upon the outcome of these brief encounters above the earth.

They were conducted rather as a kind of a celestial obbligato to the deep thunder of the battles on the ground. But in 1940 the enslavement of the most civilized and liberty-loving people on earth hung in the balance while, like the legendary Furies conceived from the days of the Old Testament, the forces of evil and the forces of good struggled in the sky. The machine became as important as the man. The best of men were brought together with the best of machines and England survived. This is the story of the conception, birth, the life and the passing of the Hawker Hurricane, called "the greatest airplane that has ever flown."

It is one of man's unique abilities to create, in a sense, in his own image. Whatever he does, whatever he fashions, whether with the soul that animates him in poetry, music or painting, or whether with his hands, more than a little of himself, his nature, character and his dreams find their way into the finished product.

If even today while we are menaced by new tyrannies, we are still free and masters of our own destinies, it is because this putting of himself into his craftsmanship is peculiarly strong in the Anglo-Saxon race.

The solidity, reliability, the stamina and, over all, stanchness and ability to take it of the British people have found their way into everything they have made, whether it was a piece of furniture or a ship, or a bit of leather or fabric.

Their ships survived in battle where others sank; tables, chairs, clocks, the utensils fashioned three and four centuries ago are still as fresh and sturdy as the day they came from the hands of the craftsmen. Their houses still stand after eight hundred years; they built the automobile that never wears out; they wove the cloth that seems to last forever; they have left the imprint of their character on everything they have ever manufactured.

So did a man by the name of Sydney Camm embody something of himself, his race, his nation and his tradition into the airplane he designed for the defense of his country.

The concept of the Hawker Hurricane had existed ever since the day when in the heavier-than-air flying machine of the Wright brothers the military men had found a new weapon. This utopian dream they evolved was of an airplane so fast, so light, so maneuverable, so heavily armed that it would drive every enemy ship out of the sky. It would be both the irresistible force and the immovable body. How far from this dream were the pathetic kites made of bits of sticks, shirttails and string that engaged in their solo dogfights over France in World War I!

The story of the Hawker Hurricane began in the year 1933, in an August heat wave so extraordinary that the asphalt melted under one's boots.

Would you remember that summer? Adolf Hitler and his National Socialist party had assumed power in Germany and were rearming. Ramsay MacDonald was Prime Minister of Great Britain and Sir John Simon, Foreign Secretary. Franklin D. Roosevelt was President of the United States, with Cordell Hull his Secretary of State.

They were trying desperately to save the Disarmament Conference, which Germany was determined to scuttle. That was the year that the League of Nations received what amounted to its deathblow. Everyone was looking the other way.

There was peace. In retrospect, it seems, one should have known or guessed the black murder boiling in the heart and mind of Adolf Hitler. Yet no one did, for there was midsummer stagnation and people lolled on the beaches.

It was on one of those rare, humid, sticky days that Sydney Camm left the Waterloo train from Kingston-on-Thames and walked up the Aldwych in London to Adastral House, seat of the Air Ministry, where he gave his name to the commissionaire and said that he had an appointment with a Major Buchanan, Deputy Director of Research and Development at the Air Ministry.

The commissionaire noted the brief case which Mr. Camm carried; nearly everyone who came to Adastral House had a brief case, but he did not know that in this one was being carried the destiny of himself and every other living Englishman.

At approximately the same period, perhaps even the same week, a jack-booted Nazi, black-uniformed and decorated with what was to become the most hated symbol in the world, the Swastika, clicked his heels to Air Minister fat Hermann Göring in the Air Ministry in Berlin and announced a visitor whose name was Willy Messerschmitt.

The reason for Sydney Camm's visit was the following: the R.A.F. wanted a new and faster fighter plane. Camm (now Sir Sydney), then thirty-nine and since 1925 chief designer for Hawker Aircraft Ltd., had something to say on the subject of what it would have to be. In the brief case reposed blueprints for a revolutionary airplane.

With enthusiasm and high hopes, he entered the usual small, dingy office with threadbare carpet, dusty files and hard chairs. A tall dark man with a prominent nose, stubborn chin, determined mouth and deep-set eyes and the premature stoop of the preoccupied, he got down to business at once with Major Buchanan.

In short, sharp bursts of speech, his expressive hands shaping form and dimensions in the air in the manner of an artist, Camm read finis to the biplane as a military aircraft. For he and his associates knew that the double-decker fighter plane could not be pushed through the air one r.p.m. faster than the 250 m.p.h. they were then getting out of the Hawker Fury, which Camm had likewise designed and which was in his opinion as obsolete and useless as the dodo.

He said, "For a high-speed fighter, the monoplane is the only answer. We must get rid of struts and wire and every other drag." Blueprints came out of his brief case as he began to speak of a monoplane which they had in project at Hawker, one which in fact had been on his drawing board for three years and in his mind ever since the Hawker Fury biplane he designed had taken to the air. For like all dedicated designers, he dwelt in the present only long enough to finish a job. Thereafter his mind leaped into the future.

Major Buchanan listened to what the designer had to say. He studied the blueprints, and what they told him was both novel and startling. Here was a heavier-than-air machine with, to begin with, an air frame of totally different structure and design. If it ever got up off the ground it would fly faster than anything heretofore seen. But . . .

And in those days it was the buts that counted. Major Buchanan said, "On the whole, I agree with you, but there are two main snags in these days of disarmament. I can't see the Air Council facing up to the cost. And after all, it is a bit revolutionary, you know. All that I can promise is that I will put up the plans." And this was as far as Sydney Camm and his airplane of the future got that day with the Air Ministry, and for many another as well.

In Berlin Fate, that ironic dramatist, was sketching another scene. Herr Messerschmitt was parting from Herr Luftfahrt-minister Göring with the sum of four million marks credited to him privately for the development of his fighter plane as a part of Hitler's conspiracy to break the peace treaty of 1919 and rearm Germany with military aircraft.

It was the old and too well-known story of the difference between the totalitarian tyranny bent upon conquest and the democracies content with peace. Further attempts that Camm made to sell his airplane proved to be equally negative for many months to come. No one in the democratic Britain of 1933 wanted to talk about war or consider the cost of new weapons. But Sydney Camm never let up.

This is not to say that the Air Ministry or the Air Council of Britain was asleep, for in 1930 they had already called for a new fighter and had even admitted the possibility of accepting a monoplane, although this type of aircraft was being frowned on as "cranky." The reason they were prepared to consider a monoplane was that the Supermarine single-winged plane had just won the Schneider Trophy at the then unheard-of speed of 328 m.p.h.

It is curious that at that time Camm's designs for both a monoplane and a biplane were rejected as being too orthodox and insufficiently advanced. Actually he was then, and in one instance twenty-five, years ahead of his time. One of the criticisms made of his design was that he was tending to see the new ship as a monoplane made of steel but fashioned in the manner of a wooden airplane.

Yet Camm knew very well what he was doing. An imaginative dreamer, from boyhood on he had filled the sky with imaginary airplanes of his own design. At the age of eighteen, only two years after Blériot had flown the Channel, these dreams had taken the form of building and flying model aircraft, and as secretary of the Windsor Model Aero Club, he had built a rudimentary man-carrying glider.

Thus, in 1933, the situation was that the military could not be interested in the revolutionary new design provided by the same man who had furnished them with their best fighter aircraft, while the Hawker board never for a moment wavered in its trust in Camm and enthusiasm for his new model.

This private company decided to continue with Camm's project as a private venture, an experiment to be run parallel with another similar one, the Rolls-Royce P.V12 aero engine, which, under the name Merlin, was eventually to become the power plant of the Hurricane.

However, pressures were building up around the Air Council, headed by Lord Londonderry, Secretary of State for Air. Younger members of the Air Council staff were clamoring for a new fighter that would have to weigh as much as 6000 lbs., instead of 2000, travel at over 300 m.p.h., instead of the then top of 223, whipped aloft by an engine far more powerful than any in existing aircraft and with firing power doubled and quadrupled.

When the cost, something in the neighborhood of five thousand pounds for each ship, was mentioned, the horrified silence with which the older members of the Council had listened to these demands became vocal. The public would never stand for it, they said, and anyhow, 223 m.p.h. and the modest climb of over a thousand feet per minute of which the Fury was capable was "a rather good performance." They then had laid before them Camm's design for just such a ship as the R.A.F. was demanding.

They spent a year trying to shoot down the Hawker Hurricane before it even took off from the drawing board. The wing loading was too high, they said. Pilots would not be able to handle it; it was far too heavy; there was no existing engine that could lift such a mass into the sky; it would never maneuver.

But their technicians now began to see otherwise. They became inspired with the same faith in the Hawker design as had the board of the Hawker company. They urged the Air Council to give it a trial and finally, in February 1935, the Council gave in and one prototype, high-speed monoplane, K.5083, was ordered from Hawker. The order form, in all probability, was the usual document executed in triplicate with ifs, ands, buts and whereases, clauses, counterclauses and fine print—a piece of paper—and at the same time an instrument of execution—the beginning of the end for the Third Reich.

1935: The murdered Dr. Dollfuss, Chancellor of Austria, was already dead six months. The Nazis had an air force and Hermann Göring was its commander. German industry was working at high pressure to enlarge the Luftwaffe and the Nazis were claiming parity with Britain on the basis of a front line of between eight hundred and eight hundred and fifty aircraft. Stanley Baldwin was Prime Minister, Franklin D. Roosevelt was in his first term, and the British seemed to fear no threat to peace, even though in July Mussolini had begun his campaign against the Ethiopians. Nevertheless, Lord Londonderry, Secretary for Air, in the House of Lords, while cautioning the House against taking an exaggerated view of Germany's strength, proposed to raise the strength of the R.A.F. at home to fifteen hundred first-line machines by March 1, 1937, with an addition of two hundred and fifty more pilots, and in addition to the eighteen new stations already planned, thirteen more.

And now began one of the most dramatic races of all time, a race between life and death, freedom and slavery. The tape was the Battle of Britain, the contestants the Messerschmitt and the Hurricane. It was going on night and day while the jockeys who would ride and guide these winged steeds, the fighter pilots, were still boys in school, or grease monkeys in garages, fledglings or utility pilots hanging about country airdromes.

In the city and outskirts people went to work and came home to their rows of little suburban houses and their gardens hedged with dusty privet. Hard by one of these were the offices of the Hawker Aircraft company, on Canbury Park Road, a dingy street in Kingston near the railway line where the Waterloo trains rattled past. In Britain, the race was being run in the design office on the first floor, a long room decorated in dirty cream, with its old oak drawing boards and leaded lights. Here sat seventy-one draftsmen and in the center, in a kind of a glass cage from which he could watch every man, was the driving, dominating figure of Sydney Camm.

From time to time he would leave his vantage point, stalk up and down the room peering over shoulders, correcting, praising, and criticizing, almost with the temperament and in the manner of an orchestra leader, who must build the individual sounds made by each musician into a symphonic whole. Camm had the reputation of being something of a disciplinarian. He had no time for lack of ability or for fools. His own brain and hand were controlled; he expected the same from his associates.

A draftsman who erred would be set upon the right track by Camm personally. Now that the order for the first Hurricane had been given, there was no holding Camm. He drove his team and himself to the point of exhaustion. He had no notion of the race against time. He only wanted to see his creation take form and leave the ground. He was that kind of a man.

Four thousand separate blueprints had to be made before the Hurricane began to take shape.

On the other side of the road, in a small dingy workshop, the first Hurricane was being built in the greatest secrecy. Security was complete, not even all of the men who were working on her knew exactly what they were making, but soon there began to appear a graceful little monoplane with a fixed undercarriage to be powered by a light Goshawk engine.

There was no smooth going; snag after snag developed and was overcome. After much argument and soul searching it was decided to use a retractible undercarriage and a hydraulic system was devised instead of an electric one.

It was before the advent of the aluminum skin. Fabric had to be applied to the tubular-steel frame, fuselage and wings so that not a wrinkle would appear in the smooth surface offered to the slip stream. Sometimes such tiny irritating problems as how to make four tapering pins joining to the fuselage fix with absolute contact in the holes of the new Fury monoplane, as the ship was then called, would take a week or more to solve, but solve them they did.

In the meantime things were happening on the military end which at one time almost caused this ship, which was to mean so much to England, to become stillborn and abandoned. A battle developed within the Air Ministry on armaments. The older men of the Air Staff believed that the wing of the monoplane would be too flexible to provide a steady gun platform and were for mounting four Vickers guns in the fuselage, guns that were already obsolete. Air Marshal Sir Ralph Sorley, then at the Armament Research Establishment of the Air Ministry, thought otherwise.

Sorley wanted eight Browning machine guns fixed in the wings, four on each side, a heavy battery that had never before been attempted. It was ironic that so complete was the secrecy and security concealing the building of the Camm monoplane that Sorley did not even know that a flying gun platform capable of supporting his battery was in the making.

As usual no one would listen to him and official red tape stood between the air marshal and his need to test the new Browning battery. However, Sir Ralph Sorley was an airman and belonged to a breed that has never been shy about "liberating" material needed to conduct their business. At Shoeburyness there was a graveyard for obsolete aircraft. Although out of date, the planes were still on paper the official charge of the Air Member for Research and Development—Air Chief Marshal Lord Dowding.

Sir Ralph took his decision: to "borrow" one of these, and he still chuckles now as he recalls the incident. "I can't remember just where the plane came from," he says, "but I arranged that it should be set up on the range. Eight Brownings were put up at four hundred yards. Bursts of two seconds with solid and explosive ammunition were fired. To my joy the effect was all I had imagined. The structure was cut through in so many vulnerable places that one could safely count on two seconds as being the lethal dose. It was about then, I believe, I confessed to Dowding that I'd borrowed one of his old aircraft and shot it to ribbons."

He had to do so. Armed with these facts and photographs of the wreck that had once been a flyable aircraft, he went to the Air Council. Dowding forgave him and the Council was deeply impressed and Sorley was told of the aircraft Camm was building and sent to advise him to install his battery.

The reception he met was not exactly exuberant. Camm was the creative artist engaged in building a perfect aircraft which would outperform any known machine. Sorley and his guns were looked upon as a nuisance which would tend to blunt the beautiful dream. But Sorley was quietly insistent and Camm practical. The designer was won over and the Hurricane got its sting, the concentrated firing power of eight guns against which no German bomber or fighter was able to stand up.

Other things were happening. The P.V12, the Rolls-Royce Merlin engine built as a private venture, became a reality—and a sensational one, because it was an engine with the then unheard-of power of 1025 h.p., which, if it could be fitted to the new ship, would enable it to fly at 330 m.p.h., or eighty miles an hour faster than any other existing interceptor.

This was something to thrill the mind of a creator. Pegasus was preparing to take form and wing from his brain; here was the strongest heartbeat in the world to lift it into the sky.

Back to their drawing boards went the seventy-one draftsmen. Plans were redrawn, mechanics again swarmed over the prototype in the dingy hangar. The Rolls-Royce Merlin engine was fitted. The name Fury was dropped and the new ship was christened Hurricane, the speed of the wind with which it would sweep down upon the enemy.

Word was now seeping into the Air Ministry

that something really hot was taking shape under wraps out at Hawker. Then about this time, Junior Air Vice-Marshal Philip Joubert had become certain that a new propeller, then being produced in America, was a *must* for the Hurricane. This was the variable-pitch airscrew, which made take-off and landing safer and increased the aircraft's maneuverability and climb during combat.

He therefore sought out Air Chief Marshal Sir Edward Ellington, Chief of Air Staff, to press this modification.

Sir Edward looked at his junior in amazement. "Good heavens, man, do you not realize these things cost two hundred and fifty pounds each. It is impossible," he said.

Joubert, now Air Chief Marshal Sir Philip, recalls, "I received a good snub for my pains and I am sure that this unfortunate interview resulted later in my being sent to India to learn about 'fighting.' " The prototype remained with its old fixed wooden propeller.

On March 6, 1935, prototype K.5083 was wheeled out for its first flight.

For all of his maestro's temperament, the Sydney Camm of those days was a repressed man: aircraft after aircraft had come off his drawing board and leaped from the ground into its element and he had never turned a hair. But he confesses that only once in all those years did he feel nervous, excited or moved and this was on the morning of the Hurricane's first projected test flight. He disguised his feelings with silence and an abrupt and taciturn manner with his associates, but he admitted later, "We were all feeling pretty emotional."

The creation of an airplane is like nothing else. It will fly on the drawing board; the mock-up may be a little beauty; it will perform perfectly in the wind tunnel; the prototype resting in the field will look capable and sturdy; but what it will do in the air no man knows until it is taken there by the test pilot for its first flight.

It may obey all of the blueprints, all of the figures, all of the rules and laws of aerodynamics, or it may kill him.

The best brains had concentrated upon a machine into which dozens of new and untried factors had been built. They ought to work, but would they? For the K.5083 was now an entity, a whole. It was no longer simply a series of parts, it was a finished machine. "It" had become "she," with a personality. What would that personality be like?

The man selected to take this new, untried, extraordinary and advanced aircraft aloft for the first time was an old fox of a test pilot by the name of P. W. S. Bulman, known as George to his friends. He was a small, prematurely bald extrovert with a bristling mustache, large generous mouth and amused eyes. What was left of his ginger-colored hair formed an atoll fringe around his skull. He could add to his name the initials of the Military Cross, won flying with the Royal Flying Corps in the First World War, and an A.F.C. in the Royal Air Force, awarded when he was chief test pilot at the Royal Aircraft Establishment at Farnborough.

Bulman was now chief test pilot at Hawker.

He was that human, sensitive precision instrument, the pilot's pilot. He was neither a fool nor a daredevil; his aim in life was not only to fly aircraft but to walk away from them thereafter.

That breed of flier like Bulman, who wants to know everything there is to know about his plane before he takes it up, is dying out, but then they existed. Therefore there was a lot of Bulman in that first Hurricane.

For days during the early stages he sat in its cockpit studying new instruments, new controls, familiarizing himself with the landscape of his tiny enclosure. As an old-time fighter pilot, he had been instrumental in helping to get Camm to accept the eight-Browning battery. As one who had held enemy aircraft in his gun sight, the thought of eight guns letting go at one time fairly made him drool.

Camm himself admitted that Bulman "had helped me no end with the Hurricane." And it was at Bulman's request that a special propeller of finer pitch had been substituted to make a first take-off easier.

Yet with all his experience and his study of the prototype, Bulman was to be a pioneer on this flight, a veteran pilot and at one and the same time a student who was going to have to learn as he went along and learn quickly. He was used to handling biplanes. How would a monoplane feel, particularly a monoplane with an engine so powerful that he would be hurled into the sky at a rate never before experienced by man?

Old-time pilots flew not only by the seat of their breeches, but by ear, the sound of the engines, the hum of the wind on struts and wires. K.5083 had no struts and wires.

A pilot used to open-cockpit flying knew he was skidding by the wind on an ear. He was a part of the element he had invaded. Bulman for the first time was going into a cockpit with a canopy, totally enclosed.

The K.5083 had been sent to Brooklands Airfield under wraps at dawn late in October, where a group of greatly mystified men were waiting for it. Bert Hayward, rigger, chain-smoking, said, "This must really be something out of this world with all the hush-hush. They say old Camm has been nursing it like a newborn baby." Foreman "Bill" Bailey laughed and replied, "Oh, he always does that, but I'd go along that this is something special. I've never known them to shift a prototype at this hour to keep anyone from getting a look at it."

At that moment the big transport rounded the corner with a shrieking of brakes and pulled up. All eyes were turned to the vague shape shrouded under a tarpaulin it carried. There was no way of telling what was beneath. One thing was certain, it was wider than they had expected, in fact too wide to enter the gates.

After a quick conference the men decided that if the mystery was ever to reach the flying field to be unveiled there was only one thing to do. The gates would have to come down. After five minutes work with crowbar and spade the posts were parted and several yards of barbed wire rolled back. The transport accelerated and moved slowly into the airfield. Fate, the dramatist, watching, failed to make a point of the symbolism. This was not the last barrier the Hurricane would break in its long and adventurous career.

In the secrecy of the hangar and behind closed and guarded doors, the curious men quickly stripped off the tarpaulin and from one of them came a long whistle of surprise. "Well, that's an odd-looking thing," he said, echoing the thoughts of the others. "I wonder if George Bulman will ever fly it."

She was indeed an odd-looking ship. No one had ever seen one quite like her before. Her silver fuselage was shaped like a bullet with a hump on its back, the tail fin rose higher than the enclosed office, all of this set upon a low, graceful single wing, over which the cockpit was centered. The wing fitted flush with the fuselage. The fabric lay as smoothly as though it were her own skin; not so much as a bolthead showed to interfere with her streamlining. She was the first of the flying projectiles—always provided that she would fly.

There was many a boffin, or "back-room boy," as British scientists were called, of the experimental department at Hawker who questioned this. There were some who said she was too heavy to get off the ground at all, others that she would be cranky, dangerous and full of vices.

On paper this new ship gave the promise of leaping beyond the bounds of reality to a speed a hundred miles per hour faster than anything that had been produced before. The Schneider Trophy plane had clocked not more than 328 m.p.h. Figures declared that this new project would fly at 340 m.p.h. But only two men really believed it, one was Sydney Camm and the other, test pilot Group Captain P. W. S. Bulman, late of the R.A.F.

That morning, then, of November 6, one of the least worried of men at Brooklands Airfield was that same Bulman.

Trains were rattling by the field, carrying crowds to London, heading for Westminster and The Mall, where the Duke of Gloucester was marrying Lady Alice Montagu-Douglas-Scott. No one really paid any attention to the bright silver monoplane standing far out in the field surrounded by a little group for all the world fussing like anxious hens about one special chick.

Cars drew up. Sir Frank Spriggs, the general manager of Hawker, Sydney Camm and a group of other executives arrived. They smoked, chattered and tried not to look nervous. Only Camm stayed at little off to one side, alone and uncommunicative.

The irrepressible Bulman, in overalls and flying helmet, cracked a joke or two with them and then Bailey signaled that all was ready. He ran across the field and vaulted into the cockpit and suddenly there was no more joking. He wished to get on with the job of mastering this new bird. He wanted, once and for all, the replies to all the unanswered questions.

He slammed the cockpit cover shut, the starter

battery whirred, the propeller did one, two, three, four slow turns, and then with a rattle and roar and a gout of smoke bursting from the exhaust, the engine came alive and the first Hawker Hurricane began to move.

She was alive, yet still earth-bound as she taxied slowly to the extremity of the flying field and headed into the wind, her nose slanting into the air and her pilot seated in his strange new office atop her graceful wings, the leading edge straight, the trailing edge tapering to a rounded tip.

Bulman checked his instruments; the distant murmur of the engine rose to a shattering roar, the bellow of each of a thousand horses, and then she began to move slowly at first and then faster and faster. Up came the tail, she was rolling two wheels on the ground, and to their horror the watchers saw that Bulman was running out of airfield. Would she ever come off? Or never? Or too late?

Bulman must have said, "Come on, old girl, it's time we got up," and pulled back the stick, for to the watchers the aircraft seemed to leap into the air with curious, throat-catching eagerness.

As they stared, the undercarriage retracted and she climbed steeply. Then almost before they were aware of it the plane was mounting higher, higher, following the sound of its engine into the sky until it vanished.

It was still too early for congratulations. Only looks were exchanged. They were waiting silently and after half an hour the drone of the K.5083's Merlin engine signaled its return and the bright bird swept back into view, circling the airfield.

The wheels reappeared from the underbelly, flaps came down, she sailed across the grass, the nose rising. Three points kissed the turf in a perfect daisy cutter, the first Hawker Hurricane sighed briefly and returned to earth. She was born, she was a person.

Bulman taxied over to the waiting watchers and switched off. He leaped out of the cockpit grinning broadly, ran over, shook Camm by the hand and joked, "It's a piece of cake. I could even teach you to fly her in half an hour, Sydney."

For on this first flight he had found, as thousands of pilots were to discover later in trouble and in combat, that this Hurricane was that rare and unusual aircraft—one totally without vices.

Every question had been answered. The ship had the highest degree of maneuverability, with all the sturdiness to take and withstand the most amazing amount of punishment.

It was a safe plane to its pilots and was to be a merciless destroyer to the enemy.

Then the tension broke. There were shouts and laughter and cries of congratulations, and Sydney Camm found himself surrounded by well-wishers. He listened gravely, but when he returned to his car there was a faraway look in his eyes as of one who is dreaming new dreams, as though he had already forgotten his perfect creation and was already thinking of the new to come.

Camm now reveals what no one at that time ever knew—namely, that he himself had had a moment of doubt.

He says, "When the design of the Hurricane had

gone beyond the point of no return I suddenly had a foreboding that it would be no good. I was always a worrier. Sopwith, Sigrist, Bulman and I had all decided that strength should be an important factor in this ship, but I always had one regret.

"I wished the wing had been thinner. If we had had more time it would have been the greatest aircraft of all time. As a matter of fact, I felt that the Hurricane was already somewhat outdated back in 1937. Yet, if we had not gone ahead we should have had nothing when we went to war with Germany."

But, however Camm felt later, he had made his gift to the nation then. The Battle of Britain was less than five years away. On that day and on that field, about to be towed back to her hangar, was the instrument which in the hands of its fliers was to alter the course of history in the Second World War.

PART TWO

SYDNEY CAMM's old prototype K.5083, which never took to the air in combat or fired a gun in anger, made her first kill before there ever was any declared war or any "enemy." She achieved this by being so perfect a creation that a rival destroyed himself trying to match her performance.

The paradox of the behavior of nations is sometimes difficult to fathom. They concentrate upon the development of weapons with the utmost secrecy, behind locked and guarded doors, with cloak-and-dagger security. And then suddenly, like children, they want to show off their new toys and usually select the time and the place for this where all the international spies, military observers and experts of the world can gather to watch, the excuse being that it is a kind of international muscle flexing, designed as a warning.

In July of 1939 there was a great air show at Brussels and the R.A.F. had wanted to exhibit the Hurricane. But at this period none of the R.A.F. Hurricanes had been fitted with the new variable-pitch propeller which was so materially to improve its performance. Only the prototype, the now four-year-old work horse K.5083, had this new modification.

There were further complications, for K.5083 was a civil aircraft. Only George Bulman and Hawker's other test pilot, Dickie Reynell, could fly it and since unfortunately neither of them were in the R.A.F., they were thus not qualified to fly with the service contingent, even though they were both ex-Air Force.

However, R.A.F. types are not ordinarily stopped by anything as vulnerable as rules and regulations. The two civil test pilots put their heads together with their R.A.F. friends and went to work. Reynell, who was a reserve R.A.F. officer, was officially "called up" for the duration of the show.

The matter of the private ownership of the prototype was solved even more simply. The boys secured a couple of pots of paint and painted the R.A.F. roundels onto the wings and body of the aircraft, and for this brief period of her life and history—a life and history that had been vital to the security of the British nation—K.5083 joined the Royal Air Force of Great Britain and wore its war paint. It was while thus disguised that she made her kill.

Over the Belgian loud-speaker came the announcement. The next exhibition flight would be by the Hawker Hurricane of the British Royal Air Force.

A buzz of excitement ran through the throng packed into the grandstands, gay with the flags of all nations whipping in the breeze. Then the excitement died to a hush of expectancy.

There was a stir too among the members of the military missions gathered from all Europe, and the German and Italian contingents went on the alert. For this was the aircraft they had come to see.

On this show at Brussels hung the whole weight of British prestige in the air at a time when the warmongering Hitler had swallowed Czechoslovakia and Austria and threatened Poland, and the Luftwaffe of Air Minister Hermann Göring was throwing its weight around.

The military men of Europe and, in particular, the smaller nations waited anxiously to see whether Britain had an answer to the challenge.

That answer stood in the shape of a tiny silver monoplane with the red and blue roundels of the Royal Air Force painted on wings and fuselage.

Behind the ropes erected to keep spectators at a respectful distance were Dickie Reynell and George Bulman and a half dozen British mechanics apparently going quietly about the business of last-minute preparations for take-off. And not a single person in the vast crowd so much as suspected that these men were facing failure and defeat at that very moment.

The most ignominious fiasco that can take place at an air show was in their minds. In all likelihood their aircraft would never get off the ground.

For the starter battery provided by the organizers of the show was for only twelve volts instead of the fourteen required to activate the Hurricane's powerful 1250-h.p. engine. Unless the heart could be set beating the bird would never take to the air.

How cool, ordinary and normal everyone looked as beneath that concentrated gaze Reynell climbed into the cockpit and the starter battery was wheeled out on its little wagon and connected with the aircraft. In their mind's eye both Bulman and Reynell were imagining what would happen when the too weak battery made contact—a low hum, an explosion, a flash of blue flame, a puff of gray smoke, and then the announcement over the loudspeaker, "Ladies and gentlemen, it is to be regretted that owing to technical difficulties the Hawker Hurricane will not fly."

But there was nothing to do but try. Reynell called for contact. The heavy propeller turned over once slowly—far too slowly.

In the cockpit Dickie Reynell, perspiration streaming from his brow, strained on the electrical booster.

Standing on the ground George Bulman, the man who had nursed this same Hurricane through its official birth years before, felt the starter cable growing hotter and hotter in his hands. The inevitable catastrophe which follows overloading electrical equipment was only seconds away.

And then the Hurricane came through. By all the laws of mechanics, engineering and electricity she ought not to have started. But she did!

The big blades did two more flips; the engine coughed and fired with an echoing ear-shattering roar.

Reynell winked at Bulman, and a few minutes later he was airborne.

As though to celebrate the life that now throbbed through her, old K.5083 chinned herself on her new prop, pulling herself aloft.

Then she threw herself about the Belgian sky with all the abandon of a joyous bird. Dickie Reynell was giving the Germans and Italians, and all the rest gathered below, the works, but the old prototype seemed to respond as she never had before, rolling, diving, spinning, looping, and doing everything but turning cart wheels.

A murmur from the crowd rose again. The German and Italian contingents tried not to be caught exchanging glances with one another.

These men already held in their brains the secret of the war they were about to launch, and what they saw was sobering, for they were mentally measuring speed and maneuverability against what they knew of their own Messerschmitt 109.

As a grand finale Reynell put the sturdy little ship into an outside loop, and as she climbed to the top of the rim of the circle the Hurricane suddenly shot bright streamers of orange flame backward from her exhaust, drawing a gasp rising almost to a shout of astonishment from the crowd.

The Germans and Italians no longer concealed their amazement. They were not only astonished but rocked. What had the British come up with now? Some new booster? A secret fuel injector no hint of which had reached them through spies or leakage? The climbing silver ship, trailing its tail of fire, looked like a comet.

How were they to know that the Hurricane was pulling their legs and that the unexpected pyrotechnics was nothing more than excess petrol whipped from the carburetor by the negative pull of gravity.

Dickie Reynell came floating home to a great roar of applause and cheering, and setting the old girl down sweetly and neatly, leaped from the cockpit in an offhand manner.

The Nazi fliers took off in their Jungmeisters, determined to uphold the myth of the superman, or at least to put on a performance that would take some of the edge off the British show. They had the guts, but the point was, they did not have the machine.

One of the Germans, trying to emulate the incredible almost vertical climb of the Hurricane, stretched his own ascent beyond the limits of what had been built into his aircraft. He stalled, spun, crashed and died.

What an irony that the very first kill of an enemy that the Hurricanes were to encounter hundreds upon hundreds of times, in skies ranging over half the surface of the earth, should be accomplished by the first prototype of this great war bird ever to take to the air.

But this kill and performance of the Hurricane is ahead of its time and we return to the days of the infancy and fledgling period of this aircraft, newborn in 1935. She was the creation of Sydney Camm, but George Bulman had helped her into this world with the brilliant midwifery of his piloting on her first flight.

Today, twenty-five years later, all that Bulman remembers of that first flight is the sweetness and the confidence the ship inspired in him.

Used as he was to open cockpits he was also conscious of a kind of claustrophobia under the hood of the streamlined monoplane, and he remembers being delighted some days after the first flight, when the hood suddenly blew off over Cobham and was never seen again.

He also missed the revealing music of the wind on struts and wires, but he recalls being well aware of the enormous gulf that had been bridged and that he had taken part in the birth of a new era.

He also harked back to a day of sheer horror, when he was called upon to perform before a committee of VIPs before the final acceptance of the Hurricane by the Air Ministry as an R.A.F. fighter.

T. O. M. Sopwith, then chairman of Hawker, had invited the Air Council and high-ranking airforce officers to Brooklands to see the Hurricane in flight. Lord Swinton, the Air Minister, was among the top brass expected.

With that perversity which sometimes dogs a project that is to have such a vital effect upon millions of lives, it rained all the night before, and when Bulman arrived at Brooklands he found the flying field, which in those days was not properly drained, waterlogged. The odds were one hundred to one that, instead of viewing a demonstration of the greatest technical advance in aircraft construction since the days of the Wright brothers, the Air Council would be edified by seeing the stubby little silver monoplane nose into the ground and tail in the air, or over on its back with pilot Bulman disconsolately hanging upside down in his straps.

But, as was to be so characteristic of her, odds were nothing to the Hurricane, or difficult situations, or the untried, or apparently insurmountable obstacles.

Odds of a hundred to one? What then was the one chance? In this case it happened to be a single half-dry, almost firm, narrow strip less than a hundred yards long which Bulman had located in the midst of the morass. If she could manage to pick up speed on that she might get into the air. And to make matters worse, by the time the VIPs arrived, the wind had changed, forcing a cross-wind take-off if the strip was to be used.

The kind of pilot George Bulman was would never have attempted to take an airplane off on that day. But canny flier though he was, Bulman had already succumbed to the extraordinary confidence that this airplane inspired. And for this reason alone he climbed into the cockpit to have a try.

He gave her throttle. She moved slowly as mud sucked at the wheels. The Hawker people watched with their hearts in their mouths. The VIPs looked on with the cold eyes of men charged with responsibility who would accept no excuses, only results.

Then the Hurricane seemed to lighten herself and run along as if on tiptoes. She found the dry strip, lifted her tail and roared down the field. It was less than her normal take-off run, but at the end of it she leaped from the ground as though animated by a will of her own. Once she was clear, the sweating and amazed Bulman hung on her prop and took her aloft. The VIPs nodded their heads sagely and England was saved.

Seven months later Hawker received an order for six hundred "Fury Interceptor Monoplanes," as the prototype was called. Three weeks later, Camm suggested the name Hurricane to the Air Council and it was accepted. By October 1937 the first production Hurricane L.1547 was airborne.

If the winner was in production, so too was the loser, for in Germany likewise the die was cast, and pouring off the assembly lines was the Messerschmitt 109.

In the meantime, the pages of history had been turning with ever increasing tempo.

King George V had died—the air-minded Prince of Wales became king and a year later was to abdicate. The Cunard liner *Queen Mary* was launched. The day was to come when each time she thrust her bows outward-bound from New York Harbor she would carry an entire division, men who would help to turn the tide on the ground, as the Hurricane would stop the Germans in the air.

In Germany the Nazis were in full cry; the Nazi-Fascist axis was a reality; Germany and Japan became allies; German aircraft and pilots were gaining experience with the Spanish Fascists in Spain. On Sunday, March 13, 1938, Hitler rode through the streets of Vienna, and the Anschluss was a *fait accompli*. Munich and the occupation of Czechoslovakia were just around the corner.

It was in 1938 too that the Hurricane outgrew her adolescence and came of age, when Fighter Squadron 111 at Northolt was equipped with these aircraft, and shortly afterward Squadron 3 at Kenley also received these machines.

And on February 10, 1938, in the company of Squadron Leader J. W. Gillan, one of the new fighter Hurricanes had herself an astonishing adventure in heretofore unprobed realms of time and space and shook the world with the marvel of her accomplishment.

With Gillan and the Hurricane it was love at first flight. When it was decided to equip the eighteen regular pilots of Fighter Squadron 111 with the new aircraft Gillan, made squadron leader, brought the first production Hurricane to Northolt himself.

Gillan, then thirty-one, the son of an R.A.F. padre, had been the best pilot of his term at Cranwell thirteen years earlier.

He was an airman in every sense of the word and in the Hurricane he recognized the machine that would fulfill him.

Before he would let any of his pilots touch her, Gillan spent many a long hour alone with his Hurricane and she willingly gave up her secrets to this master pilot.

Alone with her in the sky three miles above the earth he learned when to be gentle, when to be firm and uncompromising, what were her capabilities, and what might be her limits, and here it was that he was given a glimpse of potentialities, skills, and latent power that had been built into her, which would some day enable him to astonish the world.

The new Hurricane was not easy on her masters. She demanded skill, patience, and, above all, men who were pilots and pilots who were men.

She presented many problems to iron out. Speeds and altitudes had to be determined at which flaps and undercarriage should be lowered coming in to land. For the first time in history pilots had to contend with the higher force of gravity, since pulling out too sharply from a dive could cause the pilot to black out, and unless experience enabled him to cope with this wholly new situation, he would fly himself into the ground.

A satisfactory method had to be found to prevent pilots from forgetting to lower their wheels coming home and setting up an expensive and ignominious fireworks display as the belly of the aircraft struck a trail of sparks from the ground.

The enormous increase in instruments and controls needed a long and complicated series of checks, which the flier had to make both before take-off as well as before landing, and these had to become wholly automatic to the man. For example, it was so easy before take-off to select "wheels up" by mistake and suffer the public humiliation of having the aircraft sinking slowly to the ground as the undercarriage collapsed like a hen prepared to hatch out an egg.

Gillan brought on his squadron slowly and carefully, each pilot receiving personal instruction before being permitted to take his ship off the ground. As a result the accident rate in his squadron was low and pilots were imbued with tremendous confidence in their machines from the start.

Common sense might decry this, but often there was something almost mystic in the attachment of plane and pilot.

While basically and structurally this was the same airplane that had been transported under tarpaulins from Kingston to Brooklands that October in 1935, actually this aircraft had been modified again and again, tarted up like a debutante for a party. Armor plating, metal skin, bulletproof windscreen, weather instruments, new gun sights, improved hydraulic retraction for undercarriage, had all been added.

This was the dream ship introduced to the R.A.F. pilots at Northolt, most of whom were veterans of the Hawker Fury biplane. In a sense it was something like taking a slightly stodgy middle-aged burgher away from his comfortable middle-aged wife and turning him loose with an eighteen-year-old redhead eager for life and love.

But the new girl friend was not all sweetness and light either. There were tragedies too. Men flew themselves into the ground in a dive blackout; and three pilots killed themselves sideslipping into the ground during take-off while practicing night-flying.

As in all love affairs there followed moments of disillusionment. "Old boy, she is a killer. Take it from me. There I was, upside down and nothing on the clock. . . ." Horror stalked through the squadron until a few more hours on the new ship and remedy of the defect that caused the three deaths quickly restored confidence.

And more than confidence—the rebirth of affection. For it was not the Hurricane that was guilty of these deaths after all, but a fault in the gyroscopic horizon, which was quickly corrected.

On February 10, 1938, then, at five o'clock on a cold, damp, stormy day, Squadron Leader Gillan and the station adjutant stood by a silver Hurricane on the tarmac at Turnhouse Airfield, outside Edinburgh, 327 miles away from Northolt.

The aircraft was a service Hurricane fighter which had just been delivered to Squadron 111 and which Gillan had taken north on a routine testing flight to get acquainted.

Up to that moment the plane had been untried, but in an hour and fifty minutes of bucking head wind from Northolt to Edinburgh, aircraft and man had learned all they needed to know about one another. For while two aircraft are never exactly alike, the basic qualities built into the Hurricane remained constant and never altered. And it will be remembered that, while learning to master his first Hurricane, pilot Gillan had had a glimpse of potentialities far beyond anything yet dreamed of by man in this new dimension.

The adjutant said, "You'll certainly have a tail wind to help you along, but the weather is filthy for flying."

Gillan only grinned at him, for he was in the

grip of his dream now. "Right sort of day to show off what the Hurricane can do. . . ."

Down at the end of the field he revved his engine and was happy with its song; then, clamping his log to his knee and receiving permission to take off, he climbed aloft into the windy turbulence.

Just below the cloud level he roared back over the airdrome and signaled: "Swallow to Control: setting course 167. Out." And as he said it he pressed the button of a stop watch. The time was 5:05 P.M. exactly. "Back before dinner," he thought. "Easily. Make it some time after six." He noted the hour in his logbook, then, climbing steadily through the thick cloud, he let oxygen hiss into his mask.

The Hurricane was content at 15,000 ft. It was almost as though she had read the pilot's thoughts, for Gillan was saying to himself, "We'll stick at 15,000 ft. That's about the best height for the Hurricane."

They leveled off, and here, had the Hurricane been animate, she would have expected the throttle eased back to the comfortable cruising speed assigned to her; instead, the throttle lever was jammed hard against the bar wide open.

And now the air speed began to creep up. The needle quivered a notch, and then another, past normal. The storm gods were bang on her tail, huffing her along still faster. The Hurricane was not used to this treatment and began to bounce and bump like a buckboard on a rutty country road.

The aircraft had no way of knowing that Gillan

was bent upon unrolling a strip of the map of England beneath him faster than any man had ever done before.

In fact, metals, wires, pistons, propeller, electrical systems and aerodynamic design were being called upon to withstand speeds and stresses to which they had never before been subjected and which probably only their designer, Sydney Camm, had known they could resist.

For the man there came a momentary break in the clouds.

It disclosed a large town, the fingers of factory chimneys reaching in the sky, a dark thread of river. According to time elapsed, no large town, no factory chimneys, no river should have been there. Yet below was—Newcastle.

Gillan looked at his watch and made his fifth calculation on the pad. It showed that he was doing well over four hundred miles an hour.

Back into the thick, boiling clouds they went, and now ice added to the hazards. The leading edges of the wings were shining with it and a rime had formed on the cockpit hood. Gillan muttered to himself, "You'll just have to take it, old girl."

Now the engine began to protest too at the brutal treatment, and oil fumes seeped into the cockpit.

Through two more breaks in the cloud Gillan pinpointed other towns that should have been still miles to the south of him. His calculations were so unbelievable that he threw them out as the aberrations of a man drunk on oxygen. For they said that in the last few minutes he had been traveling over five hundred miles per hour. The smell of oil was becoming overpowering and heat was coming back from the engine as well.

The Hurricane was taking a terrific beating.

Sucked onward by the relentless pull of her Merlin engine, pushed and hustled from behind by the tail wind, pounded and buffeted by the turbulences within the gray, swollen storm clouds, the aircraft shuddered and groaned, bumping and pounding until it seemed that the tortured wings must be torn from the fuselage.

That they remained there was due to the fact that seven years ago Sydney Camm and his team at Hawker had dreamed, designed and built them to stay.

The agony the aircraft was undergoing now was reflected in Gillan, who said to himself, "Oh Lord, I'm going to be sick."

But the Designer of man as well as the designer of machines had not shaped His creation to lose heart, quit or fail. In this, as it was to be all through their long relationship, man and machine were worthy of one another.

Gillan fought off nausea and fatigue and continued his battle of the controls. He was still on course, but his aircraft was now bumping and shaking so badly that he was sure he must fly the fabric from her wings or injure her beyond recourse. Plane and man continued to respond to what had been built into them.

Gillan was starting down now, putting his plane into the dive for London like a sprinter going all out for the tape. He was no longer a lone man. He was one with his wings and he would live or die with them.

The clouds thinned again, a sight forced the cry from his throat. "Impossible. It can't be London."

And then in the dusk he saw lights reflected from the surface of the twisting silver river that was the Thames. He banked steeply to the right wholly instinctively. He looked again at his watch, and with a sinking feeling at the pit of his stomach decided that it must have stopped.

There was no other explanation. For below was the bowl of the Northolt airdrome, the railway line, and the intersection of the West Road, and the dial of his timepiece read five fifty-three, exactly forty-eight minutes from Turnhouse.

"Swallow One to Control," he mumbled over the R.T. "Orbiting Northolt."

He got back a long whistle over the R.T. "Control here. You've been stepping on it haven't you? Permission to land, Swallow."

When Gillan set his aircraft down and taxied over to the hangar, the whole squadron was there to greet him; already the news had leaked out that "Gillo" had done it.

For a moment the squadron leader remained seated in the cockpit. He was sweating and trembling still from his effort and wondered why his gallant ship was not doing likewise. He marveled at the quiet except for the ticking of the cooling engine. So as one had he become with her during this fantastic flight that for the moment he thought of her as human as himself.

Then Gillan climbed down from his aircraft holding his watch to his ear to make sure that it was going. He said, "I don't know, blokes, but I think we've broken a record of something. I shan't believe it until I've worked out some figures."

And after that there was no holding the story. Within a few hours it was all over the world, despite the fact that Gillan did not wish it broadcast, the Hurricane being still on the Air Ministry's secret list. And certainly he did not want the publicity.

For publication, at that time, the Hurricane and he had flown the 327 miles at an average of 408.7 m.p.h.

What has never been revealed before is that, owing to his inability to believe that he was actually over London, he overshot the airdrome, which robbed him of an even better time.

The true facts were, as he admitted later, when the aircraft came off the secret list, that his correct time from Turnhouse to Northolt was the incredible average of 456 m.p.h. And at one point the aircraft had touched 550 m.p.h.

In all his utterances Sir Sydney Camm gives credit solely to the men who flew his Hurricanes, but if ever there was a feat to thrill the heart of a designer, it was this.

Some of that same confidence expressed by her pilots now ran through the Air Ministry at this demonstration of perfect collaboration between pilot and aircraft.

It was just as well that this was so, for there was no mistaking the truculence emanating from Germany. And the Air Ministry, now thoroughly sold on the Hurricane, ordered a thousand of them to be delivered as speedily as possible, with further modifications increasing the speed, armor, and fire power.

To assure swift production, a Canadian car and foundry company of Montreal was licensed and the Hurricane was put into production with the Gloster Aircraft Company in England.

These are simple words and facts being set down here; decisions of intelligent men. Mark them well, for they saved the life of England.

When war broke out on September 3, 1939, four hundred and ninety-seven Hurricanes were in the hands of the most skilled and aggressive pilots of the day. A month from the declaration, the first Hurricane came from the assembly lines of the Gloster company and from then on muscle was added daily to Britain's air army.

The days of the "phony war" were at hand, when raids were few and boredom was the fate of the Hurricane pilots detailed to protect Britain, even though by the end of September, Squadron Leader "Broadie" Broadhurst, then in command of Squadron 111, flying shipping patrol out of Acklington, in Northumberland, knocked his first Heinkel out the sky over British soil.

But all during these days Hurricane pilots were filling their logbooks with new evidence of the shocks this amazing aircraft could withstand, a forecast of its behavior when it was to undergo its greatest test.

In 1940, Flight Lieutenant Ben Bowring, commander of B Flight in Squadron 260, drafted to protect convoys and the naval base at Scapa Flow, while based at Skitten near Wick had a small adventure, after which he went on living on time loaned to him by the Hurricane he had taken up for a test flight.

"Testing," to the young fighter pilot of those days, meant escorting his airplane up five or six thousand feet and then "beating up" the dispersal hut or the mess hall in a terminal velocity dive—if possible, with white compression streamers trailing from the wing when the aircraft pulled out of the dive.

Of course the pilot blacked out during this happy maneuver. While pulling out of his dive at something over five hundred miles per hour and no more than semiconscious, Bowring was jerked back into awareness by a violent blow administered to the Hurricane, as though by some giant fist striking the port wing.

What had happened was that the left-hand oleo leg of his undercarriage had loosened and slipped down where, caught in the slip stream, it had been wrenched fully back, pulling the wing far out of alignment with it.

Any other airplane would have shed the damaged wing and most would have disintegrated, killing the pilot immediately. Bowring's Hurricane continued to pull out of the dive and went on flying. The pilot came out of the black-out, spent a moment marveling that he was still alive and then, turning to practical matters, found that the Hurricane would respond if given plenty of right rudder to offset the damaged wing.

With his undercarriage wrenched out of shape, he aimed for a landing on the mud beside the runway. Even at the low landing speed of a hundred miles per hour the lopsided aircraft remained airborne and floating, until, the speed dropping still lower, it stalled, cartwheeled three times and came to rest upside down and still intact.

Bowring was released from the straps that held him in and was lowered to the ground completely unhurt and thereupon issued an unsolicited testimonial to the Hawker Hurricane. He said, "That aircraft's a bloody miracle."

The annals also reveal that about the same time an Australian pilot, failing to carry out all the required checks, tried to take off his Hurricane with his propeller in "coarse" pitch. The machine failed to rise, kept on going and crashed into a hangar at the end of the field.

The aircraft plowed through one galvanized-iron side of the hangar, shedding its wings and tail as it went. The fuselage emerged from the other side, winding up in a sand pit. Rescue squads and fire engines arrived prepared to fight their way through flames to extricate a very dead pilot.

There were no flames and no corpse. The pilot, except for a single cracked vertebra, was unhurt though somewhat dazed.

Both these incidents were indicative of another trait of the Hurricane for which the pilots who flew her were deeply grateful. In crack-ups or crash landings, though shot to ribbons, she rarely caught fire.

Yet for a time, the airplane did suffer from a fire hazard that was often fatal for the pilot, but again it was shown not to be the fault of the Hurricane.

Just forward of the cockpit instrument panel there was a small gravity-feed petrol tank known as the header tank, which was filled through a trap in front of the hood.

For some reason never adequately explained, ground crews, after refueling the aircraft, would forget to replace the screw cap. And this appeared to be characteristic of some of the best crews and they were all superb, particularly during the first few years of the war.

The consequences for the pilot were harrowing. As he pulled back the stick, tilting his Hurricane into a steep climb, petrol would come pouring out from behind the instrument panel, drenching him and setting him up as a human torch.

More petrol came streaming out from the filling trap and ran down just behind the exhaust manifolds, which were hot. If the pilot, ignorant of the cause of this petrol bath, gave way to panic and reacted by hurriedly closing the throttle, the sparks thrown back by this action set aircraft and human ablaze.

If he avoided this trap, circled his Hurricane and came in to land, its steep angle of glide caused further cascades of petrol to flood the machine, and as the wheels were lowered, the petrol blown up from the floor owing to air rushing through two inspection holes, penetrated behind the best-fitting goggles and blinded the pilot.

A number of men were killed in this way, although there were several who managed to land their Hurricanes safely by throwing back the hood and putting their heads out over the side.

When reports of these disasters began to come in, Hawker eliminated the danger by fitting the petrol tank with a spring-loaded cap which snapped back into place. But no one ever discovered why this oversight used to occur among the crack ground crews.

As has already been indicated, the characteristic of the Hurricanes and their pilots which was to be of such inestimable importance was that neither gave a damn for the odds against.

There was never a time at the beginning of the war when there were not more Messerschmitts, Junkers, Dorniers and Heinkels than there were Hurricanes.

The Germans had not only the weight but even more speed, for the twin-engined M.E.110 was some thirty miles an hour faster than the Hurricane.

Yet during these early days of the phony war in France, Hurricanes were securing some decisive victories against odds of three and four to one.

It was the dash of British pilots which sent them hurtling with amazing recklessness into German formations, but it was the greater degree of maneuverability and superior armament of their Hurricanes that enabled them to get away with it.

Genuinely one—in total union with his aircraft —the British pilot felt almost invulnerable.

In the early spring of 1940, the Germans invaded Denmark and Norway, and the British reacted by putting an army ashore in Norway, with Hurricanes and Gloster Gladiators for air cover. The landings in Norway were a forlorn hope, with too few too late.

On June 2, 1940, fighting a two-day rear-guard action to cover the withdrawal of the British Army from Norway, the Hurricane and Gloster squadrons flew seventy-five sorties, fought twenty-four engagements, brought down nine enemy aircraft without a loss and beat off every attempt of the M.E.110s to dive-bomb shipping congregated at Harstad.

After the evacuation was completed, the Gladiators went home to their aircraft carrier, the *Glorious,* at sea off Norway. But what about the gallant Hurricane squadron which had given the Luftwaffe such a bloody nose? The instructions given Squadron Leader K. B. B. Cross, commander of Squadron 46, was to destroy the airfield and blow up the Hurricanes.

He was given one other alternative, almost laughable in its unlikelihood. At the extreme northern tip of Norway "there might be a tramp steamer." If they could fly there, find it, get themselves down, take their planes apart and stow them on board . . .

The same anguish that filled the heart of the cavalryman when forced to destroy his horse now gripped Squadron Leader "Bing" Cross and his pilots. For like so many who flew this airplane, they had begun to endow it almost with human qualities and certainly they felt human love for it.

And to destroy or abandon these aircraft while there seemed a hope of saving them was simply unthinkable to these men. One night Cross put to his pilots a third alternative no one seemed to have thought of.

As a result of the conference the next day, Cross thumbed a ride in a Gladiator and was flown out to the aircraft carrier *Glorious*, where he proposed to her captain, G. d'Oyly-Hughes, D.S.O., D.S.C., R.N., that he and his pilots fly out to land on his ship.

The fact that no one had ever landed a Hurricane on the postage-stamp-size flight deck of the carrier did not bother Cross.

What he put to d'Oyly-Hughes was a calculated risk. If they succeeded, well and good; if they failed, well then they would have carried out orders and destroyed ten British fighter planes.

In this case, the pilots would most likely be lost too, but every single man had volunteered without hesitation.

The captain of the aircraft carrier sparked to this idea, but there was, he pointed out, one serious and practically insurmountable snag.

The Hurricanes had no arrester hooks on their tails to catch the cross-deck cables on the *Glorious* and bring them to a halt. How, the captain asked, did Cross propose to halt them on his flight deck after landing?

Cross did not have the faintest idea and merely

replied, with complete confidence, "Will you leave that to me, sir?" And d'Oyly-Hughes agreed.

Back in Bardufoss, Cross and New Zealand-born Flight Lieutenant Pat Jameson put their heads together for hours. The result was to provide a strange task for the pilots. Equipping themselves with spades, they filled sack after sack with sand, which they strapped to the rear of the fuselage beneath the tail surfaces of their airplanes. The additional weight would hold the tail down as the Hurricanes hit the deck.

Now this was madness. A lot of mathematics goes into an aircraft. Page after page is covered with figures controlling wing loading, balance, list, and so on. Tamper with them and down out of the sky comes your airplane. It was crazy, but remember there was love involved, and also these were not ordinary aircraft, these were Hurricanes, and their pilots knew and trusted them as they did members of their own families. They simply knew the Hurricane would do it.

Ten of the most senior pilots were to take the wild gamble, and Pat Jameson was picked to go on the first flight of three, while the remaining seven would wait for a radio signal from him from the *Glorious* before taking off. If there was no signal— well, there would be a quick torch. Hurricanes could also burn.

In the clear, cold arctic midnight of June 17, 1940, the three Hurricanes, their tails dragging, somehow staggered off the ground and went wobbling off into the sky. The first part of the miracle devised by Cross and his faithful Hurricane had been accomplished, but what was to follow was still more incredible.

Could there ever have been three lonelier, more desperately worried or more gallant men alone in that night sky, flying over the sea in overweighted, unbalanced airplanes in which they proposed to do something that had never been done before? For not only had the Hurricanes never attempted a deck landing, neither had the pilots. Navy pilots had to train for months to hit that tiny, narrow, moving landing field without a mishap and in planes built for the job.

These three men were going to do it right the first time out, and not even in daylight, but in the doubtful light of the arctic night—or else.

Bang on the spot of the rendezvous they saw the two slow Swordfish planes that Captain d'Oyly-Hughes had sent aloft to guide them in; and far below, so tiny as almost to be laughable, the landing field of the *Glorious* steaming into the wind.

What followed could have been accomplished only by men filled with the utmost confidence in the airplane they were flying. The Hurricane was being asked to transform herself on the instant from a hawk to a sea bird.

Jameson went in first. He lost altitude slowly, feeling the response of his Hurricane to the loss of flying speed. He was asking her the question and she was answering it. She still responded, when any other aircraft so tail-heavy would have stalled and spun in.

Jameson approached now from the stern almost level with the deck, nose high, and then, just as it seemed that he would crash into the deck, he gave his Hurricane one burst of power to lift her, like a good jockey helping a gallant mount over a jump. She rose! Jameson cut his engine immediately and sat down. The Hurricane rolled, but the heavy sandbagged tail held her and she stayed put. It had worked. The Hurricane had done it again!

The other two, following his tactics, came in safely, and a moment later, brushing off the congratulations, Jameson was rushing for the radio room and the wireless officer to signal Bing that his plan had worked and to come a-hellin'.

By one of those mishaps that always takes place in a war, the message never reached Jameson's commanding officer and back in Bardufoss Bing Cross sweated out the hours until the silence must mean but one thing. His pilots and their planes were in the drink.

Yet there was always that forlorn chance that they might somehow have made it. He put it to his pilots. They could destroy the remaining seven planes, or "have a bash." Which was it to be?

Shortly afterward, seven more ungainly, overloaded Hurricanes wobbled into the air.

At three o'clock in the morning they spotted the clumsy Swordfish planes waggling their wings and with a thrill realized that Jameson must have made it, and within twenty minutes they were all "home and dry."

The impossible had been accomplished. The gamble had succeeded.

The Fleet Air Arm crews were as delirious with joy at this great feat as were the ten pilots. For to them this sensational night deck landing by the hottest plane then in the air meant that now perhaps the Admiralty would give the Fleet Air Arm the fast planes no one thought they would ever be able to use.

The jubilant Hurricane pilots were desperately tired, having had no rest for more than thirty-six hours. They had a quick tot or two and then were off to bed. For eight of them there were fewer than twelve hours of life left.

The tragedy that followed on the afternoon of June 8, and which, in addition to the death that came to so many, brought to naught this incredibly gallant and successful adventure in the life of the Hurricane, was one of the saddest stories of the war.

The German battle cruisers *Scharnhorst* and *Gneisenau* were at sea in the vicinity and caught the *Glorious* apparently with bombing planes on deck waiting to take off. This was the impression given by the Hurricanes parked there.

Their first hurried salvos found the target and the aircraft carrier began to burn. For two hours she was a blazing torch, alight from bow to stern.

Then, at last, with a final great sigh of hissing steam, she rolled over and sank. With her went the Hurricanes, 8 of their pilots, and 1105 men.

If two of the Hurricane pilots were to escape it seemed almost just that they be Bing Cross and Pat Jameson, the two determined men who had planned and succeeded in the attempt to bring their planes home. Somehow they managed to swim to a Carley float with three sailors—a float that eventually held more than thirty survivors.

For three days and nights in that fearful cold the men remained freezing and clinging to their last hope.

One by one they died of exposure or, in the brief periods of darkness, slipped silently into the freezing sea.

When at last they were picked up by a Norwegian ship, only Bing Cross, Pat Jameson and five other men were left alive to return to England.

PART THREE

AUGUST 15, 1940, AND SUPPOSEDLY the beginning
of the end for the British, the sweeping away of
those little shopkeeping, fogbound islanders who,
already shattered and defeated on the ground, still
dared to oppose themselves to the destiny of Nazi
grandeur in the air.

Thus the Nazi pilots saw it as their black air
fleets came roaring out of the east at the beginning
of Hermann Göring's *Adlerangriff,* or Eagle Strike,
destined to wipe out the last of British resistance
to the Führer's dream of the world of the superman.

Out of the east they came, darkening the sky and
filling it with the arrogance of their chatter over
the R.T.s of their Messerschmitts, Heinkels, Dorniers, filling it with gibes about the *feige Engländer* and *englische Schweinehunde.*

They were fearless enough at that point, for
they were young, puffed up with the myths of the
superman and swollen with pride of the power
their endless echelons represented. They were gay
and even joyous, for they were coming not to die
but to kill.

One formation, as it crossed the coast line more than one hundred strong, was heard to joke about the *Mücken,* or English gnats, that rose to meet them, a few pitiful Vs of tiny monoplanes, Hurricanes and Spitfires, that would be swept out of the sky in short order.

Thus in every age has Goliath sneered before his downfall. For the next moment the Davids were among them with their deadly slingshots—eight-gun batteries of machine guns—blazing, twisting and turning, flashing through the German formations, wrecking them fore and aft. And suddenly the air was filled with masses of twisted metal and mangled supermen, no longer proud aircraft, but debris falling from the sky.

They were a part of three air fleets that had been assigned to knock out Britain's air defenses on the ground and in the skies and soften up the island for the final Nazi invasion. . . .

Luftflotten 2 and 3 were stationed in Holland, Germany and France, Luftflotte 6 was based in Norway. Between them they could put some 2780 bombers and fighters in the air.

Against them, the British air marshals, who were to maneuver in the greatest aerial chess game ever played, had no more than 560 Hurricanes and 330 Spitfires, of which about one third remained in reserve. Thus even before the game began the Germans had four and one half times as many pieces on the board as the British. Yet the easy victory of which they were so certain was snatched away from them almost before they knew what struck them.

If it looked easy to the Germans, how did it appear to the British, with their meager resources and nonexpendable defenses?

Across the map table in the cavernous underground operations room of 11 Group at Uxbridge, three quiet, handsome girls of the Women's Auxiliary Air Force were moving small wooden disks representing reports of minor enemy raids developing.

The controller, sitting in the gallery above, looked down upon this scene as though he were perched at fifty thousand feet in the cloudless, sunny skies of that fatal day for the German Eagles. The picture was clear to him. These were no more than nuisance raids, feints intended to draw his precious squadrons into the air before the main raid developed.

His dire responsibility was to see that his Hurricanes encountered the massed enemy fully fueled and armed. For the useful life of a Hurricane in the air was no longer than the capacity of her fuel tanks and ammunition belt. The one mistake the British could not afford was to have the Germans met by aircraft with ammo expended and petrol running low. At the same time they must not be caught on the ground refueling and rearming when the bombers came over.

If the defense was like a chess game, where moves have to be thought out five and six in advance, it was also like fencing. To every attack there must be a lightninglike and stunning parry and riposte.

At a dozen stations ranged along the south coast,

specialists were watching radar screens resembling small television sets and interpreting the lines of oscillation and dancing squiggles of light that "blipped" and faded as the scanners picked up objects in the skies. Presently some of the squiggles lengthened and burst out of the previous patterns.

Telephones now began to ring in 11 Group operations room. The quiet, nerveless girls increased the numbers of their disks. They moved them at a faster pace. Looking down at the scene, the controller hesitated no longer. There were two fifty-plus groups of "bandits" shown now over Calais and Gravelines. The enemy was gathering his forces.

The controller picked up the phone. Twenty-four Hurricanes from Squadrons 501 and 615 had already been scrambled from Gravesend and Kenley and were hauling themselves steeply into the sky. As they did so, the unruffled voice of the controller came over the R.T. "Vector 132—buster. One-hundred-plus bandits approaching Dover."

This was the arrogant Nazi horde joking about the English gnats coming to meet them. The Hurricanes changed course and headed for Dover with every r.p.m. their Merlins could churn up.

As 501 approached Dover the leader spotted twenty black planes with wings in the shape of a flattened W heading toward them and slightly below. They were Stukas. Instantly the squadron went into line astern and attacked head on, roaring through their ranks with all guns firing.

As the formation of Nazi bombers fell apart and began to dive and tumble from the sky, the Hurricanes turned steeply, then put their wings over and fell among them in a running fight in which fourteen out of the twenty were destroyed or badly damaged. The price paid for this was two Hurricanes shot down, but the pilots bailed out. Remember this last item.

The Kenley Hurricanes were less lucky. B Flight was caught still climbing by six M.E.109 fighters. Pilot Officer Truran was hit by a cannon shell. Injured, his Hurricane on fire, he yet succeeded in landing his aircraft safely. And this is another item to be remembered too, for as it was in the beginning, so it was to prove throughout. You are watching developing before your eyes, as it were, the pattern of the winning of the Battle of Britain.

The 109 that got Truran didn't last long. Flight Officer Eyre and Pilot Officer Lofts shot it down into the sea.

It wasn't all money-for-jam. Reports poured in at an ever increasing tempo. Interceptions were not always successful. Lympne Aerodrome had been put out of action for two days and Hawkinge Aerodrome damaged.

But there was no time to worry over minor Nazi successes. For more than an hour the radar tracking the enemy showed massed blips of a great attack now developing far out over the North Sea and approaching the east coast from Norway, Göring's one-two punch.

Warned in time, 13 Group had scrambled five squadrons and these were now patrolling the coast. Eight miles out of sea from Tyne, the Hurricanes of Squadron 607 from Usworth sighted sixty-five Heinkel 111 bombers escorted by thirty-five Messerschmitt 110 fighters flying banked up almost a thousand feet in a broad reversed-wedge formation.

Pouring down out of the sun, Squadron 607 shot down eight bombers and its appearance was such a complete and stunning surprise that the bombers panicked, broke formation, jettisoned their bombs and fled. Instead of the intended pattern-bombing of Tees and Tyneside, only a few houses in Sunderland were destroyed.

The Luftwaffe command was counting upon their estimation that by this time the British fighter forces would have been committed beyond recall and that the east-coast fighters must be on the ground refueling. It therefore sent fifty JU 88s from Aalborg in Denmark to bomb fighter airdromes in the Hull area. These bombers came unescorted by fighters, so certain was their commander that the earlier raids would have thrown the defenses out of rhythm.

But Hurricanes of Squadron 73 were already patrolling a convoy off Hornsea. The controller of 12 Group assessed the German intentions properly and directed Squadron 73 to intercept and attack the Hun off Spurn Head. Seven JU 88s went down in flames and the formation was broken up as once again the ambush caught the enemy unawares.

In these two engagements on the east coast alone, General Stumpf, commanding Luftflotte 5, had lost a third of his bombers and a fifth of his long-range fighters to those pesky gnats, the Hurricanes.

The British suffered reverses. Driffield Aerodrome was damaged. The fighter station at Martlesham was attacked and Hurricanes of Squadron 17 were almost caught on the ground. The Rochester area was heavily bombed because four Hurricane squadrons were misdirected owing to a faulty radar plot of a previous raid departing from Martlesham.

Squadron 111, the first ever to be equipped with Hurricanes, got into a bitter battle when Luftflotte 3 launched the biggest raid of the day, a bomber formation of one hundred and fifty strong escorted by a large number of fighters. The squadron fought the Germans all the way from the coast to Rochester. Hardly had it landed to refuel and load fresh shells when it was scrambled again as Luftflotte 3 launched eighty dive bombers and fighters in a raid against the south coast. Squadrons 249 and 32 were also scrambled to meet this attack and the battle was fought over Portland and Selsey Bill.

The Germans attacking the Portland area withdrew with heavy losses, but the fury and crescendo of the great struggle increased as the enemy attempted desperately to expose the left flank of Fighter Command and destroy its airdromes.

Again and again German raids of between eighty and one hundred and fifty bombers protected by single- and twin-engined fighters pressed ever further inland, aiming at the destruction of Croydon, destroying buildings and two aircraft factories. But still the Hurricanes, those indestructible gnats buzzed about them, took their toll and prevented them from wiping out Croydon and the airdromes southeast of London.

The Hurricanes took on any odds—three to one, four to one, ten to one. They seemed to be guided by one gigantic will, setting up a wall of fire through which the arrogant Germans could not wholly penetrate.

High above the bomber fight at 20,000 ft. some thirty Messerschmitts prepared to overwhelm and destroy the half dozen Spits sent up to oppose them. No matter what was happening below, here was one they could not lose—vulnerable British planes outnumbered five to one and with the sun in their eyes. The Germans settled themselves comfortably and with itchy trigger fingers dove onto the climbing Spits.

At this point, from 40,000 ft. out of the skies above a thunderbolt was launched upon them—a single small monoplane, a battle-mad Hurricane blasting their tails, ripping their wings from their fuselages, shooting up their pilots as they panicked and broke formation to fall victim now to the waiting Spits.

Where did this devil come from? It was like something out of a story book, some Lone Ranger of the sky. What was this confounded plane which had been able to climb higher than any German aircraft? This was fear-making and nerve-shattering. What good was the myth now in the face of this unexpected hellion from above?

This was the spirit of the Battle of Britain. This also, as it happened, was Broadie, in his personal and private souped-up Hurricane, in which from his lair at the then unheard-of operational altitude of 40,000 ft. he either directed ambushes of his Spits, or himself dove into the brawl.

Broadie was Squadron Leader Harry Broadhurst (now Air Chief Marshal Sir Harry, K.C.B., K.B.E., D.S.O. and bar, D.F.C. and bar, A.F.C., and Commander of Allied Air Force Central Europe). A merry fellow with laugh-crinkled eyes, an impish smile and sense of humor and survivor of four serious crashes, he was as indestructible as the Hurricane which was his sweetheart and partner in action.

At the beginning of the war, after he took over command of Squadron 111, flying out of Acklington, in Northumberland, Broadie and his Hurricane had shot down the first German plane over British territory, a Heinkel.

At Dunkirk Broadhurst, by then wing commander, fought the Germans with his Hurricanes of Squadrons 85 and 87 with good effect, but at such high altitudes that the grousing ground troops did not even know they were being given air cover, leading to Churchill's remarks about the victory inside the deliverance at Dunkirk gained by the Air Force.

He said: "Many of our soldiers coming back have not seen the Air Force at work; they saw only bombers which escaped its protective attack. They underrate its achievements. I have heard much talk of this, that is why I go out of my way to say this."

When the German Army appeared not many

miles away Broadie and his squadron evacuated Lille Mer Aerodrome in a hurry. Like all good skippers, the last to leave, Broadie sent off his ground crews by transport plane and then his fighters. He made a last check, noting a few unrepairable Hurricanes burning on the ground, and then took off.

When he got upstairs he found himself alone. His command, under the impression that he was following close behind them, had departed for England.

Broadie, feeling uncomfortably nude, set off for the coast through skies swarming with German fighters. With his squadron with him he could have fought his way out of anything. Alone, he was pigeon for the Germans.

Over the brown beaches of the French coast six M.E.109s jumped him. Broadie started at Page One of *Evasive Action* and went through the book, finishing up jinking like a mad waterbug only a few feet above the sea with his Hurricane depreciating rapidly.

Half his elevator was shot away, then most of an aileron went; a cannon shell exploded in his forward compartment; his canopy was shattered, and the wings began taking on the appearance of a fine sieve. The Hurricane apparently wanted to get home too, for it kept on flying, even with a bullet through its heart—the engine, from which oil, its lifeblood, was now leaking. Just as he raised the rim of Northolt Aerodrome his engined seized up, and he came gliding to earth like a flying brick.

Since the engine was dead, the Hurricane, a candidate for anyone's junk heap, stayed put at the edge of the field in which he had set her down. Broadie crawled out of the cockpit, welcomed by friends, and walked away from another landing. But as he went he kept looking back at his poor beat-up sweetheart. One doesn't leave an old tried-and-true love so easily.

Posted two days later to Wittering, in command of the Hurricane wing there, Broadie was unable to forget his old friend who had brought him safely home in the face of the worst the German fighters could do. He became moody, silent and morose. Americans would have said he was "carrying a torch." He was; but it was for an airplane.

Brooding over his abandoned darling, Broadhurst suddenly realized that as far as the Air Ministry was concerned the aircraft had been lost in France. Even the logbook, burned by the cannon-shell explosion, was missing. His pet, probably still rusting at the edge of the field, officially no longer existed, and, in fact, there was actually nothing to stop him from "liberating" that Hurricane for himself.

There are still thousands upon thousands of secrets moldering in dusty files in ministries and war departments, and every so often someone produces "the best-kept secret of the war." But one thing is certain, no one has ever penetrated the veil which shrouds the manner in which Broadhurst journeyed to Northolt, acquired and had patched up for himself his own trusted and beloved Hurricane.

Broadhurst had his initials, H.B., painted in

elegant letters, somewhat in the manner of a millionaire monogramming his Rolls-Royce, on the side of his Hurricane, and thereafter throughout the Battle of Britain he led his wing with his private Hurricane.

It was one of the peculiar characteristics of the Hurricane that she stirred the imaginations of her lovers and led them on to distant heights and along previously unknown paths. It was also characteristic that often to different fliers she suggested different uses to which she might be put, such as inspiring Britain's brilliant legless pilot, Douglas Bader, with the notion that here was the perfect aircraft for concerted attack by squadrons flying in formation, and starting a controversy as to which was the most effective way of shooting down Germans, which raged through the Battle of Britain and long after.

To Broadhurst her sweet handling qualities and broad undercarriage suggested that here was the ideal aircraft for night-flying, and with it he helped to lay the foundations of the technique of knocking the Hun out of the night skies.

This, of course, was before the introduction of radar contact, which revolutionized night-flying. Broadhurst and his pet took to stooging about over London by themselves, hovering far above the blacked-out city. Every so often a dark shadow would cross the path of the moon mirrored in the silver Thames.

Then Broadie would dive. Miss H.B.'s eight guns would chatter and a Nazi "flamer" would go twisting and tumbling to earth.

It was Broadhurst too who evolved the top-cover technique later adopted by many group leaders, the trick of hovering as high above the battle as his engine would lift him, acting as spotter for his squadrons, and then diving into the melee where speed and surprise would do the most good.

Then occurred an unexpected complication. Broadhurst was posted to the command of the famous Hornchurch wing, which by this time was all Spitfires. There was, of course, no question in his mind of leaving Miss H. B. Hurricane behind. She came with him.

Here, now, there developed another difficulty. The old girl was falling behind. It was not that Broadie loved her less, but that with her early engine she could not keep up with the newer, faster Spitfires. Something would have to be done if this beautiful romance was not to go on the rocks.

One day a high executive of Rolls-Royce Ltd. told him of the new Hurricane Merlin engine they were producing with the two-stage supercharger. Broadhurst turned on his charm, and it must have been devastating. He simply had to have one of those for his private Hurricane. Why, this would enable him to fly even higher than his Spits— higher than anything the Germans were putting out.

His request was, of course, quite impossible, except—that all the world loves a lover. Miss H.B. was missing from her usual place in front of A Hangar for a spell.

Then she suddenly reappeared with the most beautiful face lifting ever to greet the eyes of the genuine flying man. Her whole front had been re-designed and converted, obviously by pixies, to hold the new engine. She was now as fast as any existing Spitfire mark and could climb higher. The Lone Ranger in his Hurricane thereafter flew top cover for his Spitfire cowboys, where he saved the lives of many British pilots and added to the growing total of Luftwaffe casualties.

This is the purest storybook romance and should have a happy ending, with Miss H.B. eventually spending her last days somewhere near her master's estate or, at war's end, flying him down to Nice or Cannes for holidays. But this was life, and as so often in reality, the ending was one of tragi-comedy. One day a swivel-chair pilot, an equipment officer, made the amazing discovery that there was a black sheep in his flock. One of the wing's Spitfires was a Hurricane. This would never do. The Philistines went to work. Shortly afterward a message reached Broadhurst from Fighter Command to the effect that not even group captains of his standing and accomplishment could be allowed to have private Hurricanes when they were so badly needed elsewhere.

Sadly the wing raised a melancholy farewell toast that night to the memory of Broadhurst's personal Hurricane, despoiled by the "store bashers." And thereafter pure comedy took over. For, as everyone knew, no Hurricane could be transferred from one place to another without a "paper chase" of R.A.F. headquarters and Air Ministry forms.

The trouble was that no form could be found to cover the once private aircraft. Having no logbook, it did not even exist, and it had further been modified in such a manner that no bit of R.A.F. "poop" could adequately describe it. And, of course, as the crowning complication, she had the wrong engine. For many months Miss H.B. lay in Maintenance Unit while a wholly baffled bureaucracy tried to deal with the problem, until some chairborne genius solved it by removing the engine, which did have a logbook, and ticketing it for further use.

The air frame was allowed to rot and vanish from the ken of man. Broadhurst went on to his air-marshalship.

And all the time the Battle of Britain was raging in the skies over England in stepped-up attacks of ever increasing pressure designed to eliminate R.A.F. resistance by attrition if not by sheer weight of numbers. The fact that the British were still there and fighting bordered upon the incredible, so incredible in fact that not even England's friends could believe it possible.

And yet it was so, and in August of 1940 a group of American reporters was able to testify to the miracle. They were visiting a south-coast R.A.F. station and watched six Hurricanes take off for a patrol over the Channel.

The six flew in two sections, one at 12,000 ft. and the other slightly lower. Leading the lower one was young V. C. W. Badger—"Tubby" Badger to everyone in the mess. At 12,000 ft. the second section was led by Squadron Leader Tom Dalton-Morgan.

Suddenly over the R.T. Tubby heard Dalton-

Morgan shout "Huns ahead!" and looking through the multiplex hood saw the attack stepped up staircase fashion.

Instantly the two sections of Hurricanes joined into line astern and without another thought or a moment's hesitation piled into the tightly packed formation of some eighty Messerschmitts and Dorniers.

The squadron leader yelled over the radio phone, "I'll take the fighters. The bombers are yours."

Below, the Americans were not only listening but watching and saw Tubby tear into the Dorniers, damaging two or three before his Hurricane was so badly shot up that he could not continue the fight but was still able to return to the field. One of the three pilots with him was shot down, but the German formation broke up and turned back.

Dalton-Morgan picked out a Messerschmitt which was making a nuisance of itself flying in tight defensive circles. He attacked it and saw one of its ailerons cut loose and float away with his second burst. He was too busy harrying the Germans and looking after his own skin to note what happened to his victim.

The Americans saw two bombers and a Messerschmitt topple from the sky. Five out of the six Hurricanes that had taken off returned to the field. But what impressed the visitors most was that at the interrogation by the intelligence officer, the pilots claimed only one certain kill, one damaged and one probable, while Dalton-Morgan only reported his Messerschmitt as "damaged."

The reports sent back by the correspondents did much to help still the rumors that R.A.F. figures of German losses were biased.

It was true that the Luftwaffe was suffering staggering losses; yet it seemed that the day must come when the opposition would be overwhelmed, when the great Nazi bombing and fighter fleets which were to pave the way for the invasion would no longer be met by those vicious little craft that kept plunging into their formations, shooting them down or panicking the "brave" Nazi bombers to the point where they were jettisoning their bombs long before target and turning tail.

But still the Hurricanes, with their deadly armaments, continued to rise from Uxbridge, Biggin Bill, Northolt, Gravesend, Kenley, Lympne, Usworth, Driffield, Croydon, Redhill, North Weald, West Malling, Duxford, and other airfields which constituted Britain's shield. Where did they come from, these phantom ships that saved England?

The answer to this is the untold half of the secret of the winning of the Battle of Britain. It is the triumph of the durability of the Hurricane. Teamwork made her, the effort of many men of integrity went into her, but her basic design and strength issued from the brain of one man, Sir Sydney Camm, and it was a perfect creation appearing upon the scene at the right moment.

The epic of the men of the Battle of Britain, the "so few" to whom there is still so great a debt, has been written. But this is the story of the other member of the team, the airplane herself.

England entered the Battle of Britain with 560 Hurricanes and 330 Spitfires, against three German air fleets that could put 2780 bombers and fighters in the air. After two months Nazi figures said that the R.A.F. was totally destroyed. The Hurricanes simply gave the lie to them.

In disposing of an air force there is a twofold objective—to kill the pilot and destroy the machine. The human being, in terms of personality and the man-hours of training needed, is more difficult to replace than the aircraft.

The Spitfire, the Hurricane's great rival, was the swift, dashing, eye-catching attack plane, the slender arrow that flashed to its mark, and it played its role. But the Hurricane was a defensive fighter, a work horse which by virtue of its unique combination of aggressive as well as defensive armament not only shot down more German aircraft than all other defenses put together, including ground fire, but saved the lives of most of its pilots and her own usefulness as well.

She would hold together long enough to enable her pilot to bring her home to be patched up by the superb teamwork of ground crews who would have the shattered Hurricane air-worthy within forty-eight hours, or she remained aloft at least long enough to enable her pilot to hit the silk, float safely to earth, pick up another Hurricane out of stores and be flying again within twenty-four hours.

But there is yet another facet to the many-sided

story of the virtues of this remarkable airplane. If battles are won on combativeness, initiative and courage, more than half of this impetus is supplied by the confidence man reposes in his weapon.

The old half-comic phrase "he drew his trusty sword" has a solid foundation. In fact, the ancient fighter did trust his sword; he knew its edge and temper and that in the heat of battle it was not likely to let him down.

An infantryman who dislikes his rifle and knows that it has a trick of jamming under certain conditions is less than half a warrior. The tank commander trusts his shell of armor and within it ventures boldly into the hottest fire.

Up to the time of the Battle of Britain no better extension of man's lethal aggressiveness in a new dimension of the upper air than the Hurricane had ever been devised, or one that gave its fighter more confidence and feeling of security.

All weapons, in a sense, are an expansion of man's physical person. The sword lengthened his arm; the spear extended it still further. The arrow enabled him to kill a hundred yards away from his person; gunpowder finally enabled him to destroy an enemy out of sight, until today the rocket will work his will five thousand miles away.

But the airplane was more than merely the deliverer of a long-distance bullet or explosive charge. It was a metamorphosis of man himself, which permitted him safely to enter another element.

Just as when he went into a submarine and the waves closed over his head, he became a fish, so when he climbed into the cockpit of an aircraft and took it aloft, he changed into a bird. The wings were like his own arms, the engine that powered them, his own heartbeat.

Inside this mock eagle he could hurl himself about the sky, sail, swoop, dive, soar into the sun, climb through the highest clouds.

But he also suffered from the vulnerability of the bird, that swift, feather-light creature which could be brought broken and tumbling from the sky with no more than a single shotgun pellet.

To hold a man airborne the aerodynamic design of the aircraft, a combination and balance of wings, power, tail, surfaces and actuating wires and machinery, controlling ailerons, rudder, flaps, and so on must remain intact. Destroy any one of these and, theoretically, down comes the machine. The point of this tale of British achievement was that the Hurricane somehow managed to defy the calculations, blueprints and all the rules of flight as well and remained aloft, often half shot to pieces by machine gun or cannon shell. On fire, or with great holes blasted through the wings, she still flew.

The confidence and freedom from anxiety with which this airplane inspired her pilots cannot be overestimated in analyzing this British triumph in the face of almost insuperable odds.

Courage and bravery in the face of death is a variable thing. No man could become an R.A.F. pilot who was not courageous and aggressive or who had not shown that he was willing to accept the chances of combat to the death.

But it is also known that every man, even the most gallant and daring, fights better with a valiant and trustworthy comrade at his side, or when he feels that his weapons are *superior to that of the enemy*. The legends down through the ages of the invincible and irresistible sword and unpierceable armor are evidence of the warrior's yearning for some such added security in battle.

In a measure far beyond any heretofore provided by any fighting airplane, the Hurricane was just that, a friend and comrade in the lonely skies, stanch and strong, who would not let him down and endowed, it seemed at times, almost with miraculous powers to hold together.

Her armor plating provided the pilot with added protection and there was no question but that she was the superior weapon. Nothing opposing her in the air in those days could withstand a two-second burst from her eight guns well and truly aimed.

To what extent exactly these characteristics contributed to the effectiveness of the British pilots over the German in the Battle of Britain, it is not possible to say—since individuals differ—whether 25 per cent or 50 per cent, but one thing is certain and statements gleaned from pilots when it was over, and in later years, bear this out: the confidence with which the Hurricane imbued her fliers was of the utmost importance and may well have represented the difference between victory and defeat in this struggle that meant so much to free mankind.

Listen to Wing Commander R. R. Stanford

Tuck, D.S.O., D.F.C. two bars, who joined the R.A.F. in 1935, when, as he put it, it was rather an exclusive club.

Tuck had been a Spitfire pilot, but on September 9, 1940, he was given command of Squadron 257 at Martlesham, flying Hurricanes. Of this change-over he said: "My reaction to my first flight in the Hurricane after the Spits was not good. She seemed like a flying brick, a great lumbering stallion. It nearly broke my heart, because things seemed tough enough without trying to tackle M.E. 110s in a great heavy kite like this.

"But after the first few minutes I found the Hurricane's virtues. She was solid and it was obvious she'd take a devil of a lot of punishment. She was steady as a rock and was a wonderful gun platform. The visibility was far better than in the Spit. The undercart was stronger and wider and that made landing a lot easier. Somehow she gave the pilot terrific confidence. You felt entirely safe in this plane.

"Look at what happened to me on June 21, 1941. I was flying alone on a routine patrol. I'd gone to Southend without seeing anything. I suppose I was dreaming. I'd been twelve months without a break and it was a good day. I flew on out to sea at a thousand feet. I was perhaps a hundred miles out.

"All I saw were white clouds, then suddenly shells came ripping through the cockpit and engine. The plane started rocking, my ears were hurting me. . . .

"I pulled up quickly and was immediately hit

from the left. The throttle lever was blown out of my hand. The reflector plate exploded and a chip of it lodged in my head. The door and hood blew off. The engine was missing badly and I'd no throttle. . . .

"By now my engine was spluttering and cutting out. Temperatures and pressures were climbing fast. The radio was dead and speed was falling off rapidly. Oil and glycol were drenching my legs. The plane stumbled on. The punishment these Hurricanes could take! The air frame could stand almost anything.

"My starboard aileron fell off and flames started to lick round my boots. I bailed out, shed my boots and chute and got my dinghy inflated. Shell splinters had punctured the dinghy. Two hours later a coal barge from Gravesend picked me up. . . ."

Typical of this unconquerable combination of tenacious man and nigh indestructible machine is the "incident" of twenty-three-year-old Flight Lieutenant J. B. Nicholson, V.C.

Scrambled over Southampton, August 16, 1940, the day after the Hurricane had inflicted the first severe defeat upon the Luftwaffe, Nicholson, who had not yet had any air combat, was jumped by an M.E.110 at 18,000 ft. and hit by four cannon shells. One shell shattered his hood, sending splinters into his left eye, another, entering the cockpit, tore away his trouser leg, wounding him in the heel, and the third exploded in his spare petrol tank and set the Hurricane on fire. Man and plane were as good as destroyed.

Instinctively Nicholson turned away to evade

further hits and suddenly found the M.E.110 in his gun sight two hundred yards dead ahead.

By now the Hurricane was an inferno. The instrument panel was shattered and in the heat the plastic curled like toffee. The temperatures mounted. Disintegration, unconsciousness and death could be only a few seconds away, yet the Hurricane continued to fly in a straight and deadly line, closing on the M.E.110 at 400 m.p.h., and Flight Lieutenant J. B. Nicholson continued to fight.

To keep his feet from burning he scrunched up his six-foot four-inch frame and tucked them under his parachute. Then he pressed the gun button. As he did so, with a curious sense of detachment he watched his right thumb boil into white blisters in the heat. His left hand, holding the stick open, was burning likewise. What interested Nicholson, however, was that the M.E. was twisting and turning to avoid his bullets and that his Hurricane, as though by an instinct of her own, was following the evasive action. He realized he was still moving the stick himself.

Shocked, wounded, bleeding, fried, his aircraft nothing but a flying cinder, Nicholson shot the German dead and down.

And still his miraculous Hurricane held together. She had accomplished that for which she had been built and had made her kill. Now she was giving her man his chance for life.

Dazed, Nicholson struck his head on the hood as he tried to bail out. Then, throwing it open, he fought against the straps holding him in the cockpit. One burned through and broke; he managed to undo the other and headfirst dived free.

He landed in a field near a cyclist. When he looked at his watch the glass had melted, the strap was a charred thread. But it still ticked and was still doing so three months later when he was awarded the Victoria Cross.

The archives are filled with hundreds of stories of examples of the appalling damage this warplane could receive and go on flying. And in the hearts and minds of many hundreds of middle-aged men in Britain today there is still the memory of the great love they felt for this stanch partner, which, wrecked, racked, shattered and tattered, still got them home safely.

In the great battle to save Croydon and other important airdromes near London, three pilot officers, Debenham, Blair and Smith, returning from successful attacks against the Nazi bombers found themselves jumped by Messerschmitts when they were out of fuel and ammunition and were shot up.

Debenham, who had been scrambled at Dover, had caught up with a retreating Messerschmitt and chased it all the way across the Channel, shooting it down over the French coast. Trying to get back to his base, the Messerschmitts ganged up on him.

But *all three men survived; all three men landed their beat-up planes* and turned them over to the marvelous ground crews, who worked twenty-four hours a day to patch up the battered aircraft. Shortly after, the three Hurricanes, which no doubt the German pilots had written off as destroyed in their reports, were back in the air and fighting once more.

Pilot Officer Wlasnowalski of Squadron 32, scrambled too late and caught climbing, was caught and attacked by nine German fighters.

Trapped in the lethal net made by the crisscross of tracer bullets, incendiaries and cannon shells, he seemed marked for disintegration and death. Yet his Hurricane held together, though the wings began to resemble a colander, and he not only managed to extricate himself alive but shot down one of the 109s that got itself in his gun sights as the Nazi came in for what he must have thought would be an easy kill. Then he landed his aircraft.

Squadron Leader Kellett, of Polish Squadron 303, plastered by an M.E.110, had part of his starboard aileron shot away and saw the fabric drift clean off the rear end of his aircraft. Both ammunition boxes in the wings exploded, ripping two holes in the wing surfaces large enough for a man to jump through. To Kellet's amazement, his Hurricane continued to fly as though nothing had happened. He evaded his attacker and made a perfect wheels-down landing at Biggin Hill.

Hurricane she was named, but Phoenix she might have been dubbed, for, like that legendary bird, she arose again and again from her own ashes, to swoop down upon the enemy.

PART FOUR

On the sweltering hot day of September 15, 1940, twelve-year-old Peter Guile crouched in a shelter trench in a Kentish hop field and looked at the sky.

It was not a quiet scene or a quiet day. The boy's ears were assailed by the sharp "spang" and "crack" of long-barreled antiaircraft guns and the "whomp" and the "cromp" of bombs exploding in the distance, but he remained unmoved and undisturbed, for this was his now normal world. He had almost forgotten that there was any other.

Within the red brick cottage at the top of the garden a woman was struggling with the weekly rations—four ounces of butter and bacon, one meager ounce of cheese, two ounces of tea, and, worst of all, no more than one and tenpence worth of meat brought in from the Argentine—that is, when the convoys managed to elude the wolf packs of submarines patrolling the sea approaches to Britain and the Channel no more than twenty miles away.

Through the window she could see the fields, parched by the driest summer Britain had known

84

in nineteen years. Girls in sweat-stained khaki bent their backs as members of Britain's 80,000-strong Women's Land Army to stooking the last of the harvest.

And above them, in the hot summer sky, vapor trails told the story of a massive turning point in the Battle of Britain.

For this was that bright, warm, sunny Sunday known as the second glorious fifteenth, when the German Luftwaffe made its final attempt to achieve the destruction of Britain's Air Force, when Göring sent over everything he had—target London and the defensive airfields ringing it.

High above the cottage the rhythm-throb of the German bombers filled the sky and then there came short bursts, sharp rat-tat-tats like strings of Chinese firecrackers going off. Down from the sky a piece of debris came sailing, a charred bit of fabric with a black Swastika painted on it, to fall into a nearby field.

The boy in the trench, along with his little playmates, was not greatly upset, for this was his England and his normal world. All unknown to him a different Britain was being made safe for his future because, so far above his head that they could not be seen in the crisscross sky with the naked eye, Hurricanes were at work.

Between 4000 and 6000 ft. above the ground was a prevailing screen of broken clouds. In and about them, above and below, raged the greatest air battle the world had ever known, with the hurriedly scrambled Hurricane squadrons bearing the brunt of it.

At eleven o'clock in the morning the first great raid of two hundred and twenty bombers of Luftflotte 2 with supporting fighters developed out of the east. And the Hurricanes of Squadrons 504, 73, 17, 253 and 501 were scrambled and sent to the coast to intercept while Spitfire squadrons helped to form a defending barrier across Kent.

Squadrons 501 and 253 made first contact and at 18,000 ft. charged headlong into one hundred and twenty bombers, breaking up the formation and shooting down two Dorniers without the loss of an aircraft. Squadron 501, a little to the rear, completed the scattering of the formation and when jumped by escorting 109s shot down three of them.

In the meantime, two other squadrons, scrambled from Debden to patrol toward Chelmsford, got into the fight hunting in pairs and diving onto Vs of bombers.

On the ground Air Marshal Dowding, maps and reports spread before him, watched the raids develop and maneuvered his thin defending lines of Hurricanes to get them to the right spot at the right moment, into the path of the attackers, as well as bring them down for refueling and reloading of the guns when petrol and ammunition were exhausted. Pilots, airplanes, engines and guns were overworked and approaching the limit of endurance of not only flesh and blood but metal, but no handicap seemed too great to be overcome.

Climbing into the brawl over Maidstone after refueling, Pilot Officer Scott found his engine boiling over before he could get back into the scrap and reluctantly had to turn and head for his base, for orders were to preserve the Hurricanes at all costs. Every one was needed. But while passing over Blackwater Estuary he saw a 109 scuttling from cloud to cloud in a southeasterly direction bent on a quiet departure from the unpleasantness created by the Hurricanes operating above. Boil or no boil it was too much for Pilot Officer Scott and he stalked it out to sea, shot it down and then landed safely at base.

As scattered parts of the German raiders still pressed onward the first of the tremendous battles developed over the heart of London.

A group of American observers, generals and admirals, hardly able to believe their eyes, watched Squadron 504 scramble and get off the ground within four minutes by the stop watch. Within fifteen minutes of the take-off pieces of Dorniers and Messerschmitts began to descend. This squadron, plunging as always head on into a huge gaggle of Dorniers, shot down five of them and damaged many others for the loss of one pilot killed and pursued the frantically retreating enemy out to sea over Gravesend.

Coming in from Northolt at 20,000 ft. a Polish squadron got into the fight, the first section diving at the rear of the bombers and then, with that wonderful Hurricane climb, pulling up almost vertically to blaze into the underbellies of the escorting Messerschmitts. The enemy turned tail and jettisoned their bombs.

At one-thirty the great raid of the day, and indeed of the war, developed as Göring figured the defenses must now be completely disorganized and threw in two hundred and fifty bombers with heavy fighter escort crossing at Hastings and Dover. Weary and exhausted as they were, ten Hurricane squadrons were thrown into the defense of London while Air Marshal Dowding ordered out five squadrons from two other groups in support. Two squadrons met the enemy over Maidstone again and shook the Nazis with the ferocity of their attack. The eight other Hurricane squadrons met the bombers over London and with renewed energy threw themselves at the enemy formations.

The Polish squadron was in the air again and attacked a three-mile-long line of Dorniers and Messerschmitts, more than four hundred enemy aircraft stepped up to a height of 20,000 ft. Squadron Leader Kellet attacked and shot down a 110; his squadron flamed two others and the shaken German bombers began to break up. Other squadrons now joined the fray, weaving in and out of the enemy formations. Anyone and everything that would fly was now in the battle.

Sergeant Holmes, having shot down two bombers over London, found himself out of ammunition and with a Dornier in his sights. He was filled with battle lust and probably, too, the sensation of immortality that comes to brave men in a fight. Unable to fire, with not a round left in his belt, he simply flew headlong into the Dornier and rammed it to death. Then he bailed out of his aircraft, landing on the roof of Chelsea Barracks, not far from his victim, who crashed on Victoria Station.

This incident would seem to be Sergeant Holmes's story, one of blazing courage and battle fury, but it is also the story of the airplane that inspired the sergeant. She had become his outer skin and in that moment of his flying into the German, Holmes knew beyond any shadow of doubt that he would not die, that his Hurricane would stand up, that she would protect him even while she was making her kill and that he would survive. And because he knew that this was so and because the Hurricane was the Hurricane, it *was* so.

An hour or so later every formation had been broken up and Canadian Squadron 1 attacked the remains of this great raid as it was retreating from London and added another six to the score. The battle was now over, except for a minor raid on the south, which was easily repulsed. Comparatively little damage had been done to London and the Hurricanes once and for all had decisively won the fight of the fifteenth of September.

In the Kentish field, Peter Guile and his friends climbed out of the trench and made for home, late for tea.

A grown man today, Peter Guile has drifted away from the children who shared that trench with him on that fateful day. "I don't know what's happened to them," he said recently. "L used to run around with all of them, but I don't know where any of them are now. It was a Whitbread hop field we were in on that day. Afterwards, when I grew up I started working for them."

But there was more to the Hurricane and its battle-winning proclivities than just the confidence it inspired in its own pilots. There was also its psychological effect upon the enemy.

For while the Germans suffered their greatest defeat that September 15, actually the Battle of Britain had been won a month previous, on August 15.

From the very beginning of that September fight the pilots riding the Hurricanes and Spitfires reported that the German pilots were losing heart. Repeatedly during its engagements the enemy formations flinched and fled. Cowardice claims more victims even than foolhardy courage, and the high losses sustained by the Luftwaffe on that day were partially due to the fact that German fighters were none too eager to join in the battle in support of their bombers. They too had a Hurricane neurosis.

It was that same neurosis that afflicts the prize fighter who has been knocked out for the first time in his life and then manages to secure a rematch with the chap who had rocked him to sleep.

He may be the bravest chap in the world—and the most unimaginative—but when he comes face to face with his opponent once more, he will be remembering that those fists once knocked him loose from his senses and can do it again. Thus he will be that much more cautious, and by that margin, likewise, be that much further away from turning the tables.

The Nazis on that second battle day a month after they had been so roughly handled by the

Hurricane and Spitfire squadrons, no longer fought with the same assurance or abandon.

They were remembering things they did not like to recall, how the Heinkels and Dorniers and Messerschmitts had disintegrated beneath the devastating bursts of the eight wing guns of the Hurricanes and how few of their pilots had survived to hit the silk when caught in full gun sight of the British plane.

When they talked in their mess it was of the way a Spitfire could be flamed or disabled when hit fairly, but that *verdammter* Hurricane not only kept on flying but would return a bellyful of lethal lead to the same pilot who had damaged it. Why hadn't someone told them what this British aircraft could do?

In the brief time during which they had tangled with her the Hurricane had become a symbol which stood by association for a flaming death, defeat and disaster.

The mere sight of the onrushing Hurricane on that second fifteenth was sometimes enough to send them into panic, as in the instance of Group Captain S. F. Vincent commanding the Northolt sector flying top cover at 17,000 ft. and shepherding his squadron below. There he suddenly found himself confronted by a formation of eighteen Heinkel 111s, escorted by a group of fighters.

Immediately, and without a moment's hesitation, Captain Vincent hurled his Hurricane and himself head on at the formation. In mortal funk the bombers broke up and showed their tails as they fled for home.

Vincent then pulled up sharply and dived onto the fighters from behind. As he did so he was amazed to see the leading 109 burst into flames and the pilot take to his parachute. In the terror of the moment the second 109 had been stampeded into *shooting down his own leader*. Vincent then attacked and destroyed the hysterical Nazi in the second 109 and chased the others out of England like a thoroughbred running a pack of curs off his territory. Hurricane at work!

When the day was over a total was claimed in Britain of one hundred and eighty-five aircraft destroyed as against forty British planes lost in the battle.

These figures were later to be amended and then reamended and in all probability the exact losses on both sides will never be known. Far more important was the fact that after the whipping of September 15 Hitler and Göring studied *their* figures for two days and thereafter decided to call off all plans for the invasion of Great Britain.

Physically as well as psychologically the Hurricanes, the Spitfires and the men who flew them had beaten the German Luftwaffe to a standstill. Never before had the dream of one man been so justified and probably never before as well had one fighting machine, emerging from the brain of one person, had such an effect upon the life of the people and the history of the world.

Behind the scenes, while the debris of Dorniers, Heinkels and Messerschmitts still fell on Britain, Sydney Camm, the designer of the aircraft, was working as hard as ever. The fact that he had created a flying shield for England consisting of near-perfect aircraft was not sufficient for him. For Camm, near-perfect was never a place to stop.

Sir Sydney still recalls sleepless nights spent thinking about minor details of construction or possible unsuspected weaknesses which might prove fatal to his airplane in the moment of combat or strains.

This concern pervaded the whole of the vast staff from Sir Sydney on down to the most humble workman and the airplane was constantly being put through new modifications for new means of improving its performance, trenchantly demonstrating the patriotism of private enterprise.

On the human side there was even greater sacrifice. Dickie Reynell, one of Hawker's best test pilots, and who, it will be remembered, had killed his first German at the Brussels Air Show using envy as a weapon, volunteered to fly in the service Hurricane with different squadrons against the enemy in order that he, and through him his firm, might attain a clearer picture of how the airplane performed in actual combat. By this means it would be easier for them to devise means of making the Hurricane a better and safer-flying aircraft.

This was "service" with a vengeance and Wing Commander Tuck, who flew with him a number of times, still remembers the respect he had for him as man and pilot. He recalls, "Whenever I got the chance of going from one place to another I'd fly low over Brooklands and could usually pick out Dickie on the ground. When he saw me he would scramble and between battles mix it up in mock combat."

Flying with Tuck's Squadron 43 for some weeks, Reynell not only proved himself a fine fighter pilot but an accurate and long-range extension of the eye and the brain of Sydney Camm. Reynell's reports sent back to Hawker were being studied all through the Battle of Britain and later led to a number of important modifications.

On September 9, 1940, Reynell, flying number two to Tuck's great friend Caesar Hull, became temporarily separated from the squadron during a confused brawl with a gaggle of bandits over Kent and was jumped by a large flight of Messerschmitt 109s.

With his Hurricane on fire Dickie Reynell bailed out. But he never turned in his last report. His parachute failed to open. Although he was out of ammunition Hull went to Reynell's aid and also was shot down and killed. This was a black day for the British, for Reynell was a flying scientist of the air and Hull was an ace.

The perfect fighting machine, man or airplane, is the one which not only stands up defensively under an overwhelming attack, doesn't panic or come apart at the seams and gets up off the floor when knocked down, but also has the grit and stamina to go over from defensive to offensive at the first perceptible sign of weakening on the part of the attacker.

Such machines and such men were the Hurricanes and their pilots.

When the Luftwaffe's main daylight assault

against Great Britain failed and raids began to peter out as Göring no longer cared to risk what was left of his forces, fighter pilots all over the country, hissing their favorite Huns, began asking for permission to use their Hurricanes for something they had never attempted before.

A "pursuit" ship and defensive weapon, it had heretofore taken to the air to stave off bombing attacks. Now the pilots proposed using it for attack and the carrying of the war into the occupied areas.

By doing so they changed the way of thinking not only of command but also of Sydney Camm and his modifiers at Hawker, initiating a whole new phase of life and usefulness for this durable little monoplane.

It was no more than a few months before this idea became accepted. The theory had the approval of Air Chief Marshal Sholto Douglas, who had succeeded Sir Hugh Dowding at Stanmore at the end of November 1940. He determined, with the approval of the Air Staff, to initiate a policy of "leaning forward into France." From December 1940 on, the Hurricanes carried the war into the enemy camp.

The pilots called these forays "rhubarbs."

Whence came the name, or why, or what it meant to the Hurricane jockeys remains something of a mystery, for the word, applied to action, is an American one and is baseball-writer slang for an argument or jawing match on the baseball field between players and umpire, or between players of one team and players of the other with the umpire usually in the center. This in turn was probably derived from the theatrical direction to mobs to keep saying "rhubarb-rhubarb-rhubarb" over and over again, the resulting sound being that of angry or protesting crowds of people.

But how this came to be applied to intrusions into France and the Low Countries by single Hurricanes or flights of three to six is one of those mysteries of wartime nomenclature and pilot vocabulary. Operations which involved British bombers with Hurricanes in considerable numbers flying protective cover were known as "circuses."

Our old friend, Wing Commander Tuck, took part with a pal in the very first Hurricane sortie over the Continent. The object of the operation was a reconnaissance over a man-sized slice of Holland and included Luftwaffe bases, railway junctions, bridges and factories as well, testing the German air and ground defenses and the whereabouts of AA batteries along the Atlantic Wall.

Having been on the receiving end for so long, Tuck was wildly excited at the thought of being permitted to go over and annoy the Germans—so much so that he almost came a cropper before he got across the Channel. As he tells it:

"In the first few minutes after take-off, I thought I'd have to call the whole thing off. My old Hurri was wallowing unpleasantly; she was sloppy on the controls and was near stalling. I checked my settings, engine r.p.m., flaps, etc. Everything was correct. What then was the trouble?

"I looked over to my companion cowboy and he held up one hand as he grinned at me. He extended two fingers downward and wiggled them and then he nodded in the direction of under my wings.

"My undercart! In my excitement and for the very first time in my entire career I had forgotten to retract the wheels!"

The two Hurricanes had started from East Anglia. They flew at zero feet over the sea to frustrate the Dutch-coast Nazi radar screens and maintained radio silence to retain the element of surprise.

And retain it they did, but to a degree that was almost an anticlimax to the tension they had managed to boil up between them. The Germans were so surprised at this intrusion that they paid hardly any attention at all to the two low-flying planes.

Antiaircraft guns were posted around the airfields, but only a few woke up to the British markings and fired some desultory rounds at them.

"We circled one large drome several times, and then flew at the control tower at only five feet above the grass," Tusk recalls with a grin at the memory of the astonished faces of the Germans at the wide observation windows.

Next they buzzed a detachment of Nazi troops gum-booting it along a dusty road and harried them into the ditch. The officer in charge of them could be seen shaking his fist, but no one fired so much as a pistol at them.

The pair recrossed the coast and headed for tea back home. Their own gun ports had been sealed before their departure from England, as orders were not to fire at anything but only to report on what they had seen.

This first flight of Tuck's into enemy territory set the pattern for all the rhubarbs of the future, except that the Hurricanes were allowed to defend themselves and their objectives were raised to include destroying enemy machines in the air or on the ground and shooting up airfield buildings, railroad stations, ports and communications. However, the chief motive was less to cause direct damage as to force the enemy to maintain strong air defenses in the west.

But the strange thing about these rhubarbs was that the hypnotic spell the Hurricanes seemed to have cast upon the Luftwaffe during the two great Battles of Britain and thereafter seemed to persist, for between December 20, 1940, and June 13, 1941, a total of one hundred and four Hurricane rhubarbs resulted in only eighteen engagements with Nazi fighters. It seemed as though the Hun had lost his appetite. During these sparse fights, the British claimed seven enemy aircraft against the loss of eight pilots.

Eleven circuses were flown in that same period, the largest involving thirty bombers and nearly three hundred fighters. From these eleven missions, twenty-five Hurricane pilots were lost against sixteen enemy aircraft claimed. The greater loss of British pilots was due to the fact that when forced to bail out of disintegrating or burning aircraft they were of course captured and taken prisoner.

Then, early in 1941, the Hurricane got a new job, a dangerous and almost suicidal one, but which oddly enough had already been forecast by the brilliant and gallant adventure of Bing Cross, Pat Jameson and their gallant companions in Norway at the time of the ill-fated invasion and subsequent evacuation.

She was to be called upon again as a defender in what looked to be a losing battle. Britain appeared to be in danger of defeat in the Battle of the Atlantic. Having failed to subdue the island from the air, the Nazis were now concentrating on starving England into submission with their wolf packs of submarines, supported by long-range shore-based bombers that were shattering the convoys, Britain's life line.

In March of 1941 it soon became clear that shore-based fighters were unable to protect shipping in the approaches to Britain, approaches which were vulnerable to the German Focke-Wulf Condors, operating out of Lorient and Brest and which were intercepting and bombing convoys far out in the Atlantic.

Germany's invasion of Russia only underlined this problem, for here the task was to get convoys through to Murmansk to the new ally, convoys which were out of range of any British shore-based fighters and floating ducks for the German bombers stationed in Norway.

The Chief of Air Staff went to the heart of the matter when he declared, "I am convinced that neither shore-based aircraft nor gun armament can ever secure our shipping against the scale and type of attack we must now expect. The only method of protection is the ship-borne high-performance fighter operating from specially converted ships which must accompany every convoy."

He was speaking in a sense of a dream aircraft, except that it was no dream. It existed. It was the airplane with no vices that was chosen to make this defensive vision a reality.

Two types of ships were evolved and converted, fighter catapult ships, sailing under the White Ensign, and catapult aircraft merchantmen, proceeding under the Red Ensign, but with R.A.F. defensive aircraft aboard, one to each, to be exploded into the sky when needed.

With her robustness, resistance to extraordinary shocks and stresses, and steady flight characteristics, there was only one choice of fighter aircraft for the c.a.m. and f.c. ships—the Hawker Hurricane.

The Hurricane did not let them down. Early in August of 1941, a Hurricane from the *Maplin* (which had been built only that previous April), scored the first kill by shooting down a Focke-Wulf some four hundred miles out to sea.

The first action between a c.a.m. plane, the *Empire Rainbow*'s Hurricane, and a Focke-Wulf took place on November 1. Fighter Command had provided sixty Hurricanes and their pilots who trained under Wing Commander Kirk at the new Merchant Ship Fighter Unit at Speke.

No more gallant fliers ever lived—and died—than the pilots of the c.a.m. and f.c. Hurricanes. For they knew that once they had been catapulted and were airborne out in the Atlantic, their patrol could have but one ending, in the drink. Win or lose in their air combat with the attacking bombers, when the petrol ran out, it was good-by faithful Hurricane, hello Atlantic Ocean! Hit the silk and hope to be picked up by a surface escort vessel before they drowned or froze to death!

Sometimes when the convoys went northward through the Arctic Ocean to Murmansk there was an outside chance of a landing on friendly territory—if the petrol held out.

The exploits of these rocket-catapulted Hurricanes and their pilots would fill another volume and deserve to do so. But two of these from the heretofore locked files of the R.A.F. may be looked upon as typical of this strange new partnership entered into by man and machine.

On May 21, 1942, a convoy of thirty-five ships, the largest ever to make for Russia, sailed for Murmansk. It included the c.a.m. *Empire Lawrence*.

May 25, a single Focke-Wulf Condor was sighted in the bright arctic night, circling. It was on reconnaissance, having a snoop. A bombing strike might then be expected at any time thereafter.

At 4:45 P.M. of the next day, during which the Focke-Wulf, or another, tailed the convoy, Pilot Officer A. J. Hay, a South African, sitting on the alert for long hours in his Hurricane, was just beginning to congeal when six Junkers 88s crossed the convoy at 6000 ft. and went into a line astern for the bombing run. On the radar screen further formations of Nazi bombers were seen approaching from the east. It was time for action.

Hay gave the signal for launching. He opened his throttle wide, so that his Merlin roared angrily and the tiny monoplane shook and trembled. He braced his head firmly back against the rest and tensed his stomach muscles. The *Empire Lawrence* turned into the wind. The fifteen rockets of the catapult went off with a shattering explosion and the Hurricane was blasted from the deck in a perfect take-off.

Buzzing into the air like an infuriated hornet, Hay closed on the six Junkers, which panicked into a tight V formation as soon as they sighted the lone Hurricane rising to meet them.

Hay detected that number four on the starboard side of the enemy V was lagging behind somewhat. He bore in immediately from that quarter and fired two bursts of three seconds as he came within two hundred and fifty yards of the quarry.

The Nazi's starboard engine flashed crimson; chunks of it began to fall off and drift lazily down to the frozen sea. Hay, mentally dusting his hands in a "well, that's that" gesture, left number four to its fate and turned his attentions to number two.

He gave it a five-second burst and saw his bullets go in behind the cockpit. But in the meantime, the other four Germans were concentrating their fire upon him. A cannon shell exploded in his glycol tank and he was blinded by the fumes. Another burst with a white puff of smoke against the support of his seat as he broke right in evasive action, peppering his left leg with fragments as though he had got into the way of a shotgun.

In the confusion of being wounded and half blinded, he saw another German aircraft in his sights, pressed the knob of his multiple-guns trigger and fired off the last of his ammunition.

It had been a descending battle. Hay now climbed to 3000 ft. over the convoy, enough altitude to give his umbrella time to open, informed control that he was bailing out and lingered not for a return reply prepaid.

Struggling for his life in the freezing Arctic Ocean, he found that the Hun had perforated his dinghy and it wouldn't inflate. But within six minutes, the ratings of the H.M.S. *Volunteer* had hauled him out of the sea to hot coffee, blankets and grog. Not all the c.a.m. pilots were this fortunate.

The second example of this near-suicidal type of action concerns one Flying Officer Barr aboard the c.a.m. *Empire Morn,* and his fighter direction officer, Flying Officer J. Carrique of the Royal Canadian Air Force.

This action took place in September of 1942, when a still larger convoy of twenty-nine ships was accompanied by an aircraft carrier and a number of c.a.m. ships. And there is no better way in which to describe it than to present verbatim the report of the radio conversation between Barr and Carrique.

The convoy had been under constant attack for two days and nights from both high-level and torpedo bombers and had suffered great losses. At 11:50 A.M. on the eighteenth of September, Carrique warned Barr to prepare to take off, as a group of German torpedo bombers were seen coming in from the port quarter.

The following radio conversation took place:

Carrique: We're going to shoot you off.
Barr: O.K. What are they?
Carrique: About 15 Heinkel 111s.

The rockets fired and Barr took off into a maelstrom of swaying balloon cables and "friendly" AA fire.

Barr: Stop those chaps firing at me.
Carrique: O.K., Jack. I'll do that.
Barr: Tallyho.
Carrique: Understand tallyho.
Barr: I've got one of 'em.
Carrique: Good work. Are you all right?
Barr: O.K., but out of ammunition. Did you see it go down?
Carrique: No. We were too busy dodging torpedos.
Barr: O.K. Good luck.
Carrique: Enemy aircraft coming in at two o'clock.
Barr: How many of 'em?
Carrique: About ten . . .
Barr: I'll try and worry 'em.

Barr dived into the formation, without ammunition and strictly defenseless, but the enemy scuttled off, dropping their bombs at random.

Carrique: I can't see you.

Barr:	I'm dead astern of you.
Carrique:	I can see you now.
Barr:	Will you give me my vector?
Carrique:	Vector 180 magnetic about two hundred sea miles.
Barr:	I've got sixty gallons left. Shall I try to land or shall I stick around?
Carrique:	Do as you please.
Barr:	I'll stick around.
Carrique:	O.K. How much longer can you stay up?
Barr:	About another hour. I could make that piece of land on the port side.
Carrique:	O.K., but I don't think there's an airdrome there.
Barr:	O.K.
Carrique:	Group of JU 88s ahead going away.
Barr:	I'll dive into any groups of Jerry if I see any. Then I'll try to save the aircraft.
Carrique:	Yes, good idea.
Barr:	Where shall I make for?
Carrique:	For your original destination [Keg Ostrov, near Archangel], two hundred—no—two hundred and forty sea miles away.
Barr:	180 magnetic, isn't it?
Carrique:	That is correct. I'll try and get something out for you [an escort].
Barr:	That's a good idea.
Carrique:	The wind is southeast.
Barr:	Message received and understood.

Carrique: Congratulations from the captain.
Barr: Thank you very much.
Carrique: O.K. Good luck.
Barr: Thank you. Out.

Through fog and low cloud, Barr made for the Russian coast. He landed at the airdrome at 2:15 P.M. with only five gallons of petrol left.

The Hurricane was at Malta too.

She got there by devious routes and in devious ways. There were never enough of her kind on hand.

Admiral Cunningham, Chief of the Mediterranean Fleet, pleaded the importance of Malta as a base from which to operate against the Italian lines in Africa and time and time again pointed out the necessity of air defense for the vulnerable island. Early in 1940 there were no Hurricanes that could be spared; they were needed elsewhere, in Britain and in Egypt.

When, on June 4, six Hurricanes flew for Egypt via France, Tunis and Malta, the governor, supported by the Air and Naval Commanders-in-Chief, begged that these be allowed to remain in Malta. The reply was that the fleet base at Alexandria must have priority. The top brass was squabbling over a single Hurricane as though it were some rare and precious bird. It was.

By the end of June some half dozen Hurricanes had found their way to Malta with permission to remain.

Then an overland route from West Africa, via Takoradi, was set up by which some one hundred and seven Hurricanes were got through to Egypt by the end of the year. But this was not helping Malta, which was being pressed. A faster and surer method of getting reinforcements to the beleaguered island had to be found.

Again it was the Hurricane which provided the answer. With the air operations in Norway in mind and the near-miracle of the Hurricane landing safely on the deck of an aircraft carrier, the Air Council considered that this little wonder would likewise be able to take off from a carrier if the ship could get within flight range of the island.

On July 24, the aircraft carrier H.M.S. *Argus* left the United Kingdom with twelve Hurricanes to be flown to Malta. This attempt was given the code name of Operation Hurry.

Some idea of the value placed upon the presence and services of these twelve airplanes may be gleaned from the scope of the feints and diversions undertaken by the Admiralty to cover the fact that an attempt was to be made to sneak a carrier into the eastern Mediterranean close enough to Malta to fly planes thither.

It included a sweep by cruisers and destroyers into the Aegean, and an attack and landing on Castellorizo by light forces, an air attack by aircraft of the carrier *Ark Royal* on the Cagliari airfields to discourage the Italians and a task force sailing from Gibraltar consisting of the *Argus,* the *Hood,* the battleships *Valiant* and *Resolution,* the *Ark Royal,* two cruisers and ten destroyers.

In addition, a cruiser lying off Minorca occupied itself by broadcasting false reports. No twelve airplanes had ever had such a royal and mighty escort before.

At 4:45 A.M. the *Argus* was in position to fly off her Hurricanes. One after the other the twelve roared off that flight deck as though they had never known any different take-off strip and all of them reached Malta safely. Operation Hurry was over.

But the next time that Operation Hurry was attempted, in November, it ended in a tragedy. Nine aircraft and their pilots were lost, an entire flight of six and three others.

Only four out of the first flight arrived and landed, with respectively twelve, four, three and two gallons of petrol left in their tanks.

None of the second flight was ever seen or heard from again. They had been launched too far from their objective. It wasn't the Hurricanes that failed; it was people. When their engine's life-blood of petrol gave out, the great mechanical hearts stopped beating.

The findings of a court of inquiry convened to look into the disaster have never been disclosed, but it seems to have been a combination of enemy activity near Naples, a hostile fleet consisting of a battleship, seven cruisers and a number of destroyers, and human error on the British side.

The flight crews were apparently inexperienced; there was a mix-up on the estimation of the Hurricane's range and a further one with the rendezvous with the guide planes. The Hurricanes were sent off before dawn and precious time was lost while the formation gathered. The leader of the squadron did not have the rank or experience to protest the distance they were being asked to cover. Added to this, the airplanes apparently flew at the wrong height, and the wide radiators of the tropical modification further reduced speed and range.

Control at Malta went through the harrowing experience of listening in on the R.T. as the pilots flew to their death.

In spite of this disaster and the fact of the shortage of air defenses at Malta, of Hurricanes and the overworked pilots who flew them, Malta's Hurricanes somehow managed to keep Kesselring from overwhelming the air defenses of the island. The German commander at one time threw some nine hundred bombers and fighters in an attempt to knock out the base once and for all. In three and a half months the pilots flew enough sorties to last them a lifetime and reduce their machines to junk.

Yet the Hurricanes stood up and so did the men. They kept the Germans from systematically destroying Malta's defenses.

The Hurricane moved on to Africa.

The birth of the Hurribomber, that attack aircraft which could deliver a bomb at blazing speed and fly low enough and fast enough to pitch them into road transport, was one of those fortuitous accidents in which experimental failure in one field sparks an unexpected success in another.

Some boffin in the Aeroplane and Armament Experimental Establishment at Boscombe Down had the bright idea to try to establish whether an aircraft could be used to drop bombs upon an enemy bomber air formation from above.

No specialized machines for this type of attack existed and quick analysis of airplanes available indicated that the only one with exceptional strength of wing section which might accept the burden of two 250-pound bombs slung beneath the wings was the Hurricane.

Air-to-air bombing at that period simply wouldn't work. The idea was good, but, as it developed, impractical for a number of reasons. But what *was* discovered, to the delight of the technicians and the Air Council, which had been anticipating the need for a fast fighter-bomber, was that the Hurricane, loaded down with 500 pounds of bombs, that is, a 250-pounder under each wing, handled absolutely normally under practically all conditions.

Even with only one of the wing bombs released and the aircraft technically out of balance, she would climb, dive, roll, jink and evade as cleverly as before, with her speed reduced by no more than fifteen miles per hour.

From the moment of that discovery, the fighter-bomber became a practical and tactical certainty and the Hurricane entered yet another phase of her amazing career.

But this miracle airplane had not yet exhausted the surprises she had for the nation. It was subsequently found that she could carry *two 500-pound bombs* under the wings, or 1000 pounds extra weight in all. Furthermore, in co-operation with the air experts, Hawker, led by Camm, found that it was possible to convert any Hurricane into a fighter-bomber with a minimum of fuss and labor. It could actually be done by the squadrons themselves and entailed no more than fitting a new and specially constructed pair of wings to the old fuselage.

One of the earliest Hurricane squadrons thus equipped was Squadron 80, veterans of the disastrous campaign in Greece and now operating in the desert with General Auchinleck.

Pilots unfamiliar with the virtues of the Hurricane, men who had flown prior aircraft, or had come from Spitfire squadrons, had often been critical of this airplane until one or two flips had convinced them of her superior qualities and safety factors, but now for the first time, veteran Hurricane pilots were to complain. How were they to fly a thing like that, they groused, the first time they saw the new fighter-bomber? With the bombs weighing it down it would just give the Huns a better chance of shooting them out of the sky.

As usual and as always, the Hurricane won them over in short order. After a few experimental flights they landed, rolled their aircraft up to the line and stepped out shaking their heads in amazement. For they had found that their Hurricanes had lost none of their sweet-handling characteristics and maneuverability even with a pair of 250-pound high-explosive eggs in the racks beneath the wings. Their confidence was restored. They knew that their aircraft were still more than a match for anything the Germans or Italians could put into the air against them.

Here is an account typical of an action by this squadron after it had familiarized itself with and practiced bombing tactics.

During General Auchinleck's desert offensive, Operation Crusader, Rommel was fighting desperately to save the tanks and transports of his Afrika Korps, which were streaming back from El Gazala along the road from Akroma to the coast. Squadron 80 was scrambled to help Rommel on his way.

Ten Hurricanes, among them carrying 5000 pounds of bombs, dived to attack the column from 4000 ft. Pulling up at the bottom of the dive, each pilot dropped his pair of 250-pound wing bombs into the packed motor lorries, tanks and half-tracks below.

Bombs released, four of the fighter-bombers climbed sharply to form a protective screen of top cover (now they had transformed themselves into "defensive" Hurricane pursuit planes again) while the remaining six turned sharply and came roaring down the road once more at low level, spraying the burning and exploding vehicles with machine-gun and 20-mm. cannon fire.

At 4000 ft., the four top-cover men were giving the lie to fears that the Hurribomber would be unable to protect herself. When a flight of twelve German 109Fs and a number of Italian Macchi 202s appeared to try to protect the convoy, the four Hurricanes jumped them and drove them off before they could interfere with the strafing flight. Pilot Officer Reynolds and Sergeant Mason both destroyed Messerschmitts and Sergeant Whyte claimed a probable Macchi.

The result of Squadron 80's scramble was an appalling carnage below. For more than a mile the road was strewn with blazing transport, dead Germans and aircraft wreckage. The Hurribomber had come into its own.

It was in the desert too that the Hurricane justified the use to which for a time Broadie Broadhurst had put his own "personal" Hurri, which he had flown during the Battle of Britain. At that time he had had faith that this airplane would make an ideal night fighter and had experimented with his private pet himself, stooging about in the night skies over London, even though in the dark, cloudy atmosphere of Britain the night fighter was almost blind before the introduction of radar contacting devices.

However, in the Afro-Mediterranean theater, where there would be weeks of clear bright skies lit by the glowing golden desert moon, night-flying suddenly became a profitable business for Hurricane pilots, and early in 1942, Night Fighter Squadron 73 was ringing up a regular nightly score of German intruders who because of Britain's increasing air superiority in Africa were forced to attack Army concentrations and airfields under cover of darkness.

But the Hurricane had still another amazing metamorphosis to undergo in the desert, was still to become yet another factor in the turning of the tide, was once more to take a hand in helping to reverse what seemed like certain defeat into unexpected victory.

It became apparent soon that success in conducting war in the desert depended primarily upon mobility, swift columns that knifed their way through along the few good roads. The cutting edge of the mobile column was the tank.

In June of 1942, as Rommel and his Afrika Korps were on the verge of taking Egypt and cutting Britain's life line, the British unmasked a secret weapon which did much to bring his advance to a halt and later, in 1943, during Montgomery's own forward drive, helped to break the final Axis rear-guard action in Tunisia.

That June of 1942 a column of tanks, turrets open, blond and arrogant tank commanders surveying the road ahead from the conning tower, were proceeding along a road leading to Alexandria, which shortly they expected to invest. The Nazi commander and his men were relaxed, for no British tanks were known to be in the vicinity, and they were out of artillery range and therefore wholly safe in their traveling land fortresses.

Suddenly from the lead tank went up a warning over the R.T.—*"Achtung! Jäger!"*

In the desert sky ahead, peeling off and preparing for a strafing run, was a squadron of British Hurricanes.

The tank commander rattled an order; heads disappeared, conning towers were buttoned up. To the Nazis this attack was of no more importance than a cloud of mosquitoes. The machine-gun bullets or small 20-mm. shells from the aircraft would rattle off their armor like buckshot from the hide of a rhinoceros.

The lead Hurricane flattened out its dive and roared in low at 240 m.p.h.; they expected orange fire to flash from the leading edge of both wings, but what followed was something quite different. From the head of the column came a booming explosion as the lead tank went up. The second slued around on its tracks pouring black smoke as men leaped for their lives from the conning tower. The R.T. crackled with shouts of dismay and warnings, *"Gott verdammte Engländer! Neue Waffe! Kehrt euch! Luftkanonfeuer!"*

The first Hurricane zoomed up, the second came roaring in on the panic-stricken, scattering tanks. The pilot pressed the knob of his firing mechanism and heavy armor-piercing shells slammed into a tank, penetrating it like butter and turning it into an inferno. The Hurricane trembled and shook from the recoil yet remained perfectly maneuverable under the hand of the pilot, who, aiming his flying artillery at the next half-track, knocked it out and then zoomed aloft into the steep Hurricane climb. When the attack was over, four tanks, three half-tracks and several lorries had been knocked out and were blazing, with others severely damaged, the survivors scattering for their lives.

The first squadron equipped with this new weapon was Squadron 6 and they were trained at Shandur in Egypt before being thrown into the battle in the desperate "last chance" attempt to hold Rommel at the Alamein line.

Even today this squadron, now flying high-speed jet aircraft, still proudly wears and exhibits the crest of the winged tin opener, which was to become the terror of Rommel's armor.

From June 1 to August 31 of 1942, this outfit flew one hundred sorties with its tank-busting Hurricane 11Ds, destroying forty-five enemy tanks and thirty-five other large vehicles.

Before long, as prisoners of war arrived in British compounds, British Intelligence began to learn something of the havoc and panic caused among the Germans by this new weapon.

"The first appearance of the Hurricane tank busters came as a terrible surprise," a captured Panzer man told an interrogating officer. "After they became known, they caused panic every time they dived in to attack. The trouble was, we seemed to have no support from the Luftwaffe or from our flak."

Another prisoner of war described the first attack his echelon suffered and said, "All the tank crews jumped out of their tanks in terror and stayed out until the attack was over." He too complained about the lack of cover they received from their aircraft or antiaircraft fire. But in fact, the tank busters paid a heavy price for their courage and daring. When they attacked formations defended by AA they suffered a 75 per cent casualty list, and for a time, while the Germans were licking their wounds, Squadron 6 was given a rest from this dangerous work.

But when Montgomery resumed his victorious advance into Tunisia and it was time for the kill,

Squadron 6 was called back into tank-busting service again and had themselves a day when the advance was held up on the Mareth Line and for the first time they tried an innovation. This was the use of an R.A.F. spotter riding in an armored car traveling with British forward units who directed the strikes over the R.T. where the ground commanders felt they were most needed.

On March 10, 1943, General Leclerc and his Fighting French forces were ambushed by a strong German armored unit near Ksar Rhilane. Squadron 6 was whistled up to the rescue.

Racing at the camouflaged Tiger Tanks at an altitude of fifty feet, each Hurricane opened fire at six hundred yards, closing at such speed that no more than five or six pairs of shells could be fired before they zoomed up over their targets and climbed for another run.

Altogether they flew three sorties, at 10:25 A.M., at 11:50 A.M. and a matinee at 1:25 P.M. During this time they destroyed six tanks, thirteen armored cars, ten lorries, five tracked troop carriers, a gun and a wireless van and trailer. The German surprise attack had been turned into a disastrous rout marked by the black pall of smoke hanging over the desert from the burning machines.

On March 24, and again, two days later, the squadron hustled to El Hamma, where a dangerous build-up of German tanks was threatening to hold up the advance, and led by Squadron Leader D. Weston-Burt, the twelve cannon-firing Hurricanes hit some thirty-two tanks, besides numerous lorries and mobile guns. They were congratulated by Air Marshal Tedder, commander of air forces, on a "magnificent show." Said the air marshal, "Such efforts will have a great effect on the time in which we kick the Hun out of Africa."

The commander of the ground forces concurred. On the twenty-fourth, after Squadron 6 had destroyed another nine tanks and eleven other vehicles, General Montgomery sent his "admiration and congratulations."

It was during this last attack that the Hurricane gave another demonstration of her extraordinary toughness. Warrant Officer R. J. Mercer had his starboard wing so badly shot up by enemy fire that he was forced to bellyland in the desert to prevent stalling and crashing. He walked away from the landing unhurt.

From March 9 to April 8 in 1943 this squadron of tank busters flew close to 120 sorties, firing 1230 rounds of 40-mm. shells claiming the destruction of 46 enemy tanks and 37 other guns and vehicles.

On the debit side they lost 24 aircraft crashed or forced-landed, which the Air Ministry called "an exceptionally fine dividend," for out of these 24 crashed aircraft only four pilots were lost.

No wonder these men loved this airplane.

PART FIVE

THE STORY OF the Hurricane fighter aircraft from its inception to its last flight follows no rosy path to success but strangely seems almost to imitate the pattern of great human lives, in which frustration precedes achievement and tragedies—often needless ones, or resulting from sheer bad luck— are intermingled with the success, the glory and the shouting.

The Hurricane scored more successes than any other fighting airplane either before or since, but as we have seen, it also participated in disasters and shared in the defeats which inevitably, on the side of the democracies, appear to precede final victory.

She had her place in the dramatic failure in Norway and fought valiantly in the losing cause. An entire squadron took part in the brilliant exploit of saving itself by landing on the deck of an aircraft carrier only to succumb to naval gunfire when the carrier was sunk a day later.

She fled from France with her masters, the British, when the wave of the German Army engulfed the airfields in France to the edge of the Channel, but not before she had provided valiant air cover for the retreating allied armies and the gallant little navy of small craft that plucked them from the beaches of Dunkirk.

She won her stirring victory in the Battle of Britain and suffered with the rest of the British forces in the disaster in Greece and Crete.

She was involved against fabulous odds and logistics in the battles for Egypt and Malta and took losses which would have routed the Nazis but did not perturb the British.

She was made a pawn and sacrificed, frequently with her pilot, in the Battle of the Atlantic and the vital convoy routes, when she was catapulted or rocket-exploded into the air like a guided missile with no place to come down but the icy winter sea.

She was indomitable, structurally tough, and remained airborne in the face of fire and damage, but she was not invulnerable. As the stoutest human heart fails when pierced by a bullet or the bravest man collapses under the blows of too many assailants, so too did the Hurricane come tumbling from the sky when mortally stricken and her bones still bleach in lonely places in the English countryside, almost two decades later.

Here is a sad requiem of a letter from E. F. Carter, Esq., of Hangrove Hill, Downe, in Kent:

Dear Sir:
I personally know where a Hurricane still exists although it crashed into the side of a hill about a half mile from here and was badly burned. The engine and wings and various odds and ends still lie where they

dropped and I recently removed about 30 rounds of ammunition from one of the wing boxes and safely disposed of them. If you wish me to reveal the resting place of this "Noble Lady" I will. I often wonder what happened to the pilot.

Another of the great tragic dramas in which the Hurricane was involved—in losing campaigns at first and against greater odds than ever before—was the early war in the Far East. There, she arrived not only too late with too little, but lacking any kind of protection of radar, or for that matter any other kind of warning system, and there for the first time she was caught and killed on the ground.

She was thrown into battle against not only overwhelming odds but more modern and faster aircraft in the Japanese Zero fighter and was made to fight without proper ground support.

Yet in the face of all this, on the brink of defeat, she managed to help save India as she had saved England and played so great a part in routing the Germans from Egypt.

The campaigns in Burma are known as the Forgotten War. The Hurricane shared in all the miseries and defeats of those campaigns and, in the end, no other aircraft had a more varied or decisive part to play in the final victory.

It was the Hurribomber which broke the Japanese attacks before Kohima with its precision strikes. Hurricanes softened up the road from Tiddim to Kalemyo, with its forty hairpin bends, and enabled the Army to advance.

Rocket-bearing Hurricanes (she took to rockets as she had to bombs, cannon or any other weapon with which they saw fit to festoon her) wrecked the Japanese tanks gathering for the defense of Myinmu Bridgehead and fighter Hurricanes strafed the Jap into retreat and silenced his guns at Akyab.

Hurricanes bombed bridges, dove onto Zero fighters parked on their own airdromes and destroyed them; they dropped supplies to the Chindits and laid smoke screens to cover the British crossing of the Chindwin.

On one occasion they even temporarily called off the war on the Japanese to take on another kind of winged dive bomber, microscopic in size, but much more dangerous—the *Anopheles,* or malarial mosquito.

Approaching Tamu, the foot sloggers of the Army were compelled to advance through the Kabaw, the terrible valley said to be the most highly malarial spot in the world. Its other name was the "Valley of Death."

The medics called for a mass slaughter of the insects, if the Army were to get through. The Hurricane provided the answer to the call. Two large tanks, one under each wing, were fastened to the bomb racks. For almost a week, the Hurris took off and sprayed the entire road and its approaches on either side with DDT.

The potential casualties saved by this were almost inestimable. Illness among the troops, instead of rising to a dangerously high level and one which would have been disasterous to the campaign, actually was reduced to a lower level than could possibly have been expected.

In December of 1941, when the Japanese attacked in Malaya, the situation was as desperate as it was at Malta when the Germans first turned their attention to that important base. The entire fighter strength consisted of some outdated Buffalos and machines outdated even earlier. Even in Burma there were no more than thirty Hurricanes.

Malta was only an island bastion, but Singapore was considered the keystone of Britain's eastern empire and no matter how great was the need for Hurricanes elsewhere, the demand *had* to be met there.

By July 1942, fifty-one crated Hurricanes had arrived in a convoy and some fifty more had come on the carrier *Indomitable,* had successfully flown off her decks and been thrown into the battle.

The tragedy of those dark days and one most keenly felt by the R.A.F. men of the Hurricane squadrons was that they were fighting in a hopeless cause. When the ground troops are unable to hold and defend the airfields and there is insufficient or no radar warning of enemy attack to permit the defenders to scramble, the aircraft is doomed.

At first the Hurricanes had their usual successes in the air battles over Singapore and when twenty-seven unescorted Japanese bombers appeared over the city the Hurris shot down eight of them.

The following day the bombers returned, this time escorted by Zero navy fighters. Five Hurricanes were shot down victims of the Zeros' new tactics, but above all due to circumstances beyond the control of the pilots.

At 20,000 ft. or above, the Hurri pilots had a speed advantage over the Zero. They could climb more swiftly and their power dive was faster. But they soon found that the Japanese possessed an advantage which the Nazis had not shared over Britain the previous year. There was insufficient antiaircraft opposition.

Over Britain the AA batteries had kept the Germans honest and forced them to fly at an altitude where the Hurris could get at them to greatest advantage. Any Huns who came in low were popped off by the ack-ack boys. The Japanese were able to attack at low altitudes, where they had the speed and tactics.

Even so, by adopting novel air maneuvers, such as pouring down out of the upper skies from all directions in isolated streams of fire and diving and zooming in and out of the low-flying Jap formations, the Hurricane pilots still managed to bag their quota of enemy bombers.

But the Hurricanes by themselves could not cope with the advancing ground forces of the Japanese. The Hurribombers and the types bearing 40-mm. cannons were effective against vehicles, or shipping, but not against ground troops, where heavy bombers were needed to dislodge them or pile up an advance.

Singapore fell and the gallant Hurricane squadrons were lost.

The situation in Burma was similar, where

neither the Army nor the Air Force was able to hold the Japanese advance for very long.

There was only one radar unit in the whole of Burma and this was already obsolete when the attack came. This meant that the precious Hurricanes were continually being caught on the ground and many of them were destroyed without even having a chance to rise to meet the enemy. Pilots wept as their long-awaited Hurris, just out of their crates and freshly assembled, were blasted to wreckage on the ground.

But if the Hurricane as an aircraft was adaptable to whatever theater, climate or adversary she was called upon to face, so were the men who flew her. The situation in Burma called for an immediate change of tactics, if they were not all to be wiped out.

Thus when orders were given for a scramble—and these were frequently trundled over from "ops" by a messenger on a rickety bicycle owing to the lack of telephones—the Hurricanes climbed *away* from the incoming Japanese formations until they were well above them. Then they would peel and dive, if possible and by preference head on into the enemy.

If they were not shot down on this first pass they would break away, climb again and repeat the operation. This method of fighting was successful and for a time the Japanese Air Force was frustrated over Rangoon.

The Japanese reacted violently and threw in two hundred aircraft by the end of January, most of them Zero fighters, in an attempt to secure air supremacy over Rangoon. The Hurricanes cheerfully accepted the odds of five to one against. All that 221 Group had to counter this blow were sixty pursuit aircraft, of which sixteen were obsolete Buffalos. In six days of desperate fighting, fifty Japanese fighters and bombers were shot down by the Hurricanes.

But by early March the remnant of the gallant fighter forces which had been able to delay the taking of Rangoon for two months were forced to move back, since, lacking bombers, nothing could prevent the Japanese armies from moving in. All that was left were three ancient Buffalos, four American P-40s and twenty Hurricanes. Attrition and lack of proper warning system had turned the trick as the Japanese—and the British as well—knew it must.

To complete the job, the Japs sent over a force of two hundred and thirty bombers and fighters to the Magwe airdrome, where they caught this force on the ground in a series of attacks.

One of the saddest memories of the fighting airmen of those black days and times was the spectacle of eleven remaining Hurricanes, most of them too badly damaged by bomb splinters and cannon fire to fight, yet struggling in the air and limping over to the Akyab in the hope of patching themselves up and continuing the fight. A week later they were caught there and virtually wiped out. The British fighter force in Burma no longer existed. The Hurricanes saw no more desperate days ever.

But the saga of the Hurricane in the Far East

is not yet done, for the air front line now fell back upon India. The allies were now fighting on two fronts. With the Americans having their hands full in the Pacific, India was seriously threatened by the Japanese. At the same time the sea approaches to the country had been opened up by the enemy and the fleet was now in urgent need of fighter protection against the dangerous and accurate Japanese bombers and torpedo planes and their accompaniment of Zero fighters.

The next key base which would be attacked would be Colombo and the naval base at Trincomalee in Ceylon.

Hurricanes were hurriedly sent for to defend it.

They arrived from the Middle East, Mark I and Mark II aircraft of Squadrons 30 and 261, on the carrier *Indomitable,* arriving on March 7. Squadron 258 had already been moved thither from India.

As usual, Fate seemed to conspire to put these Hurricanes on the spot. The pattern had become almost characteristic. Suddenly the destiny of men and material, indeed of whole peoples and nations, seemed to hinge upon a handful of small, camouflaged monoplanes and the young men who flew them.

Every nut and every bolt in this aircraft then took on an importance out of all proportion. Lives, treasure and political existence depended upon airplanes and their pilots standing up to it —and at the usual odds of anywhere from five to ten to one against.

In Ceylon, the task of the Hurricane squadrons

was the following: After searching for the Japanese carrier force, the heavy elements of the fleet had to withdraw to Addu Atoll to refuel. At this time, Catalina flying boats on patrol sighted the Japanese carrier force on April 4, only three hundred and fifty miles southeast of Ceylon and obviously steaming to attack the island.

With the British fleet six hundred miles away, it was up to the thin line of Hurricanes.

There were twenty-one merchant vessels and thirteen R.N. ships sheltering in Colombo, plus all of the valuable harbor and dock installations of the port, which had to be protected. Shortly before eight o'clock, the morning of Easter Sunday, a force of between ninety and one hundred Japanese 99 bombers escorted by navy Zero fighters approached the airdrome at 8000 ft.

Squadron 30 had been conducting a dawn patrol, having been in readiness since four o'clock that morning, and was almost caught out of time. Some of the ground staff had even been released for breakfast shortly before the enemy appeared. The Hurricanes broke all records getting themselves off the ground. Four were still taking off as the bombs began to fall. Several turned from their climb and attacked the Jap bombers as they dive-bombed the airdrome in line astern and one of these was crashed even before it could release any of its bombs. This was up to Hurricane standards.

Eleven enemy aircraft appeared over Colombo Race Course, where Squadron 258 was stationed. Squadron Leader Fletcher immediately scrambled his men. Nine Mark II Hurricanes and five Mark I aircraft went upstairs to deal with them.

They scattered them and then joined Squadron 30 over the harbor, where a typical Hurricane-type brawl was going on, namely, what seemed to be overwhelming enemy forces were harried, disconcerted, broken up by a few determined men clad in Hurricanes, hurling themselves head on into the teeth of the Japs with what seemed reckless abandon, but which was less foolhardy actually, since, armored and winged by their faithful aircraft, they knew what they were doing.

When it was over, twenty-three of the attackers had been destroyed for a loss of fifteen Hurricanes, and probably as many more Jap planes failed to return to their carriers through damage sustained. It was a high price to pay in Hurricanes, but their gallant intervention had again succeeded. For although some damage was done to dock installations, only two small naval vessels were sunk and one merchant ship set on fire.

But this triumph too, as had been the pattern other times, had its bitter and tragic aftermath. While the Hurricanes had prevented this Japanese attack wrecking the port and sinking the invaluable shipping tied up there, this enemy strike succeeded in locating and sinking the two British cruisers, *Dorsetshire* and *Cornwall,* which were on their way to rejoin their fleet. They were out of range of Hurricane cover.

With an attack on India in mind, the Japanese made one more attempt to establish air superiority over Ceylon while at the same time crippling the

British naval forces by an attack upon Trincomalee Naval Base on April 9.

The newly erected radar station at the base reported some sixty bombers accompanied by the same number of fighters approaching.

Stationed at China Bay was Hurricane Squadron 261. Its fifteen planes were scrambled in three separate flights of five each. One hundred and twenty planes against fifteen planes makes the odds a nice round number of eight to one against the defenders, or what the Hurricane pilots accepted as their usual handicap. Anything less than five to one against them was not considered sporting.

Six Fulmers flown off the carrier *Hermes* joined the fight and it was a beauty. The battle raged from 22,000 ft. down to 8000 ft., with the three Hurricane sections freewheeling through the Japanese formations, picking on the leaders of the V flights of bombers, flaming them, crippling them, zooming up to engage in dogfights with the Zeros, turning swiftly to support Hurricanes of neighboring flights when they were in trouble.

To the background music of the roar and whine of engines, the chatter of machine guns and the pop-pop of exploding cannon shells, the deep booms of exploding bombs and crashing aircraft, it was a symphony of teamwork. Once more, men and machines came through.

When it was over, half the Hurricanes were shot up or damaged, but fifteen Jap planes were dead, seventeen others were probables which crashed into the sea trying to regain their carriers, and nine more, driven down seeking to escape from the Hurricanes diving on them from above, were claimed by antiaircraft fire.

Dock installations were damaged, but the Japanese Air Force had suffered a defeat in the air which had the same effect upon them as had the Hurricane defense during the Battle of Britain upon the Germans. They never again attempted a large-scale attack on Indian air space.

Sing a song of heroes! Gloria! Gloria! And tomorrow forgotten!

Nothing dies as quickly as an airplane, and some of them are aged and near obsolescence before they are born. The Hawker Hurricane had a long and honorable life as aircraft go and surely the most glorious one in the history of British military aviation.

But in the year 1937, at the time the first production Hurricane, serial L.1547, with the first Merlin II engine was transported to Brooklands and had its initial flight, the successors to this airplane which in its trial by fire was to save the free world was already on the drawing boards.

Hardly more than a year after the first Hurricane had been taken aloft and given life by George Bulman, the design staff at Hawker under Sydney Camm was getting to work on blueprints for two more advanced fighters. These, to Specification F.18/37, were to materialize as the Typhoon and the Tornado.

Early in 1940, when the Hurricanes were preparing to fight in Norway and the glorious exploit of Bing Cross and Pat Jameson's landing on an aircraft carrier to save their aircraft was in the making, the first prototype of the Sabre-powered Typhoon was completed.

The Hawker Hurricanes had shown the way as bomb carriers, rocket and cannon planes. The Typhoons were armed with two bombs of 1000 pounds each, or eight rockets, and were devastating in close support, having the fire power of a cruiser.

The Typhoon came into its own during the Battle of Normandy, when at Falaise and Avranches it decimated the German armor and opened the way for the breakthrough that liberated France and Belgium.

The Hawker Hurricane was still there, likewise on D Day, the first in action, but under conditions no Hurricane had ever been called upon to face—odds for instead of against. The British had air superiority with its newer and faster ships and when the R.A.F. drew a line across Lorraine and proceeded to prang every German aircraft that dared to cross it, the Hun respectfully kept to his own side.

This was not the kind of hunting to which the Hurricanes were accustomed. Some of the pilots even longed for the good old days of five and six to one against them, where a man could play around a little and show his stuff.

The Tempest had been developed along with the Typhoon and was powered with Sabre 2, Sabre 4 or Centaurus 2. The first off the line was flown by "Bill" Humble in 1943. It attained a maximum speed of 435 m.p.h.

Now the Hawker Hurricane had once flown from Turnhouse near Edinburgh to Northolt outside London in forty-eight minutes, averaging 456 m.p.h. and at one spot hitting 550 m.p.h.

But this was while Squadron Leader Gillan, who performed this feat, was being huffed along by a following gale and was going downhill so to speak. The actual cruising speed of the Hurricane was set at between 330 and 335 m.p.h., though later models probably hit 385. The Tempest could cruise comfortably at 435 and approach the speed of sound in its screaming dive.

Within two months of the formation of the first Tempest squadron, its speed was to prove a lifesaver, for it was at this time the Nazis opened their flying-bomb offensive against southern England. Everyone knows how close the loathsome Doodlebug came to turning the tide that had begun to run against Hitler. It was the speedy Tempest that was given the task of destroying these before they could reach London and explode with tragic loss of civilian life and property. One Tempest wing alone, under the command of Wing Commander Roland Beaumont, was credited with destroying more than six hundred of these dangerous missiles.

Intone a dirge for heroes then, for so quickly are they replaced and forgotten.

On a bright autumn day in September 1944, three airplanes stood side by side on the airdrome hard by Hawker's main assembly plant at Kingston.

Roped off from the runway was a throng of spectators, workmen in overalls, military men in uniform, dignitaries in frock coats. The crowd was hushed and a curious kind of grief clutched at the throat of every man and woman present. For they were there to witness the saddest and strangest of all air shows ever held, the beginning of the end of the airplane which had saved the life of Britain.

Someone who had a sense of the tragedy underlying the everlasting drama of birth, life and death had arranged for the presence of these three aircraft at this ceremony. One was Hawker's new fighter plane the mighty Tempest, whose Sabre engine could unleash the power of 2400 horses. The second an elderly but still trim-looking Hawker Hart. And in the center, with the legend "The Last of the Many" painted on the sides of her camouflaged fuselage, stood a Hawker Hurricane.

There on the field before them all was the modern, the obsolescent and the obsolete. The Hawker Hart was dead, the Hawker Tempest was in the first brave flush of youth. The Hawker Hurricane was dying, for this was the last one ever to be made, the final one to come off the Hawker assembly line.

True, it would still escort many a Hun into the next world and leave her mark upon the Japanese before she vanished forever from the scene, but every heart among the spectators knew that her day was done, her flight flown and her end near at hand.

In France the armies of Britain, France and the United States had the Germans on the run. For the first time the glimmer of the light of victory could be glimpsed at the end of the dark tunnel of five years of war.

None knew better than those ringing the airdrome the contribution that had been made by the little silver monoplane with that melancholy legend on its side—"The Last of the Many."

Prior to the display which was to take place over the airdrome there had been a ceremony at the doors of the Hawker plant, when chairman and directors of the company, including Sydney Camm, the designer of this airplane, gathered on the dais for the christening of this final Hurricane to be delivered to the R.A.F.

A dozen or so years ago she had been a dream, an idea, a thought in the mind of Camm, the response of a man of vision and genius to a need. But, as if to emphasize the fact that this airplane, which, like Drake's little ships against the Spaniards and Nelson's fleet at Trafalgar, had proved England's shield in time of utmost peril, was the result of teamwork as well as individual brilliance, on the same dais with Camm were the representatives from Rolls-Royce, who had designed and built the great Merlin engine, the heartbeat of the Hurricane, as well as men from Rotol's and de Havilland's, who had supplied the propellers, from Dowty's, who had designed and constructed the sturdy legs of the wide undercarriage so popular with pilots, from Dunlop's, who had made the wheels and tires, and from Browning and other armament factories, who had supplied the armaments which for five years had made this aircraft the undisputed ruler of the skies.

Above this last Hurricane stretched a banner with her battle honors written thereon and the flags of the nations whose pilots had flown her.

Before the eyes of the thousands of men and women workers whose lives for the last ten years had been bound up in the manufacture of this airplane, this small camouflaged monoplane with the four cannons thrust forward like stingers from the leading edge of her wings stood as the symbol of a British weapon, designed, conceived and built by Britons, which had served as fighter, night fighter, merchant ship protector, fighter-bomber, tank buster, rocketeer and ship destroyer, which had appeared in some thirty different forms and modifications and on thirty-seven different fronts.

Taking off on wheels, floats, skis, catapults and even backward-firing rockets, Hurricanes had flown and battled from the Atlantic to the China Sea, from the frozen wastes of the Land of the Midnight Sun to the deserts and equatorial belt of Africa.

Air Forces of Yugoslavia, Belgium, Iran, Russia and Turkey had included Hurricanes, and in the Commonwealth nations Canadians, Australians, New Zealanders and South Africans all had formed and fought with Hurricane squadrons, and—not to forget—there was the famous American Eagle squadron. So too had pilots of the conquered nations, the Free French, Poles, Czechs and Norwegians, formed Hurricane squadrons and learned to love them.

Now as it was being ceremoniously retired, the ceremonial speeches droned on, probably seemingly interminable. Some listened, some perhaps not, but of the thousands attending this ceremony, of which at least half were women workers, none could remain unmoved at the thought of this brave and sturdy fighter of the air that was to be no more.

For a decade the lives of many of them had been intimately connected with this single aircraft and they were entitled to share in the pride of its achievements. Some of them knew every part of this machine, every bit of steel, wire, bolt, or rivet from end to end; others working on the assembly line had performed perhaps no more than one or two operations year in year out, yet the results showed that they had performed them well and the record of the airplane in the Battle of Britain had subsequently justified the dignity of their craftsmanship.

Not only had they built Hurricane after Hurricane, assembling her from parts and components, bits and pieces, into the graceful living thing she became in the air, but, too, they had healed her wounds and nursed her to health again when she had come tumbling from the sky wrecked but still able to land her pilot safely.

Some of them there could remember the daftest things they had been required to do and for which, so to speak, the Hurricane had held still uncomplaining. Once they were even asked to fit a Hurricane with a top plane, making it into a biplane for short take-offs in occupied territory, the top plane and struts being jettisoned once she was in the air.

There was that scheme for mounting a Hurricane piggy-back atop a Liberator to be released on the approach of an enemy aircraft.

A Hurricane was chosen for an Air Staff experiment to see whether rockets could be fired vertically from an aircraft to break up enemy formations dropping bombs from above.

Another Hurricane had submitted equally successfully to experiments with backward-firing rockets assisting take-off.

They had manufactured and assembled the famous tank-busting 11D, mounting two 40-mm. Vickers cannons and two .303-inch guns. They had adapted the wings of the Hurricane to carry a variety of loads from 500- and 1000-pound bombs to 45- or 90-gallon drop tanks, or eight-rocket projectiles which gave it the fire power of a cruiser's broadside.

From their factory and machined by their willing hands had come the seagoing Hurricanes. The Sea Hurricane I was the first deck-landing conversion; the IA had catapult spools and other equipment so that it could be exploded from the deck of a merchant ship in the appallingly dangerous c.a.m. service. The IB had deck arrester gear so that never again would pilots have to load her tail with sandbags, as in Norway, to get her to sit down on a carrier deck, and the IC was a deck-landing version with four-cannon wings, a real killer when she got into the air against bombers trying to draw a bead on convoys.

There were other experiments, too numerous to mention, all made on the Hurricane because of its reliability and the conviction that with this aircraft there was the least chance of anything going wrong and certainly hardly any of its killing its experimenter. When a Hurricane was brought forth to have some completely un-aerodynamic gadget strung around its neck or hung from its wings, perched on its back or draped from its tail, *that* battle was already half won.

And now that the spectators had all reassembled at the airdrome there was yet one act remaining in this farewell.

There stood the three aircraft, Tempest, Hart and Hurricane, and out to them strode three pilots in white duty coveralls. But at the sight of one of them, a balding man with a scrubby mustache, large nose and merry eyes, a great roar went up, followed again by a sudden and deep hush as all of those present fell under the singularly emotional spell of the realization of what he represented.

The balding man, for twenty years chief test pilot at Hawker, and now succeeded by Philip Lucas, who was to be at the controls of the Tempest, had returned for his last exhibition. On November 6, 1935, little less than ten years before, he had in a sense been the doctor who had ushered the Hurricane into the world, the first ever to take her aloft and introduce her to her life in the air.

Now Bulman had turned from doctor into priest and was there to administer the last rites to this aircraft which had meant so much to all of them. Many an eye was wet as Bulman donned his helmet. That day nine years before, he had gone out to the prototype of this airplane with a joke on his lips, for he was that kind of man. But there was no joke there now or in his heart.

The three aircraft warmed up and the voice of the Hurricane seemed almost puny against the deep-throated roar of the Tempest's 2400-h.p. Sabre engine.

The three took off and made their fly past—the yesterday, the today and the tomorrow. The air through which they flew must have been crowded with ghosts and Bulman must have felt himself flying wing to wing with his old friend, partner and associate, test pilot Dickie Reynell, who used to demonstrate Hawker aircraft with him at air displays, circuses and flying pageants before the war, that Dickie Reynell who had died flying in a Hurricane against odds of fifteen to one in the Battle of Britain as a flying laboratory and who gave his life so that other young pilots would be spared theirs.

Then, after the three had flown past the spectators, Bulman with the last Hurricane wrote a final ode in the sky to those same ghosts of the upper air, the winged and deathless men who had laid down their lives in this aircraft.

In imitation of the manner in which they had dived, climbed and twisted through the formations of German raiders massing to destroy Britain, he zoomed upward in climbing rolls, looping, stalling, flick-rolling, coming out of an outside loop to dive and flip within a few feet of the ground, then soaring again almost vertically into the sky. It was a tribute to the quick and the dead but it was also old George Bulman saying, "See here, all of you. Must you write us off? There is life in the old girl yet."

Life, yes—as in the Far East the Hurricane still fought on—but in Europe her day was done and the passing of this great, heroic machine came swiftly and mercifully but with rapidity that was almost too stunning. For, a year after that touching ceremony at Hawker, in September of 1945, with V-E Day at hand, the fifth anniversary of the Battle of Britain was celebrated in London's Thanksgiving Week with a mass flight over the city by Fighter Command, with Group Captain Douglas Bader, D.S.O., D.F.C., leading the surviving Battle of Britain pilots.

Not a single Hurricane was included in the mass formation.

Perhaps someone slipped up. Doubtless somewhere ironclad bureaucracy had triumphed over warmhearted sentimentality, for surely somewhere a faithful, trusty Hurricane could have been found to show herself once more. But the facts behind this event were unassailable. A scant five years after the battle this airplane which had taken the leading part in the panicking and destruction of Hermann Göring's Luftwaffe was no longer part of Fighter Command's equipment in Britain.

Or perhaps even then, with the battle won, there simply was no time for sentimentality or looking back to that time in the year 1933 when a certain Herr Willy Messerschmitt walked out of Hermann Göring's Air Ministry in Berlin with the money and authority to develop his unconquerable fighter aircraft while, at the same time, in London Sydney Camm and his 340-m.p.h. monoplane was meeting with rebuff.

The Messerschmitt was a mass of wreckage in the dustbin of the past, the triumphant Hawker Hurricane already relegated to limbo. Eastward from Germany, new colossi, new threats to the peace, security and liberty of the free world were already germinating even before the old ones had been wholly liquidated.

Who had time for nostalgia and a sentimental sigh for the missing Hurricane? Not Sir Sydney Camm for one. In his laboratory, on his drawing board jets were being born, vertical take-off aircraft conceived, 1000-m.p.h. battle planes designed. As though liberated of the fires of war, aviation was leaping forward in giant strides of 500 m.p.h. There was no time to pause either for reflection or tribute. The same urge, the same creative genius in Sydney Camm which had brought the Hurricane to fruition when she was most greatly needed, now drove him onward to his next design, and the one to follow, and the one to follow that.

But time itself has a way of recapitulating and as men grow older they find more strongly in their hearts the memory of the loves of their youth. Such a love to those who flew her was the Hurricane.

She was loved and trusted by every man who ever knew her. She was unique in the heavens. She had no vices. In the hands of the young men who mastered her and became her lovers she saved England and all that rest of the world which cherished the right of freedom.

She was the Hawker Hurricane.

You will also want to read:

ESCAPE FROM COLDITZ
by P. R. Reid   (G586—35¢)

Colditz Castle was the German prison camp reserved for enemy officers who had escaped from other camps. The Germans regarded Colditz as impregnable and escape-proof, yet *the men went on escaping.* The story of their hair-raising adventures makes this one of the most exciting books in years.

THE WOODEN HORSE
by Eric Williams   (BG239—50¢)'

Here is t e true story of one of the most fantastic escapes of all time. Stalag-Luft III seemed escape-proof—hedged with barbed wire, guns, S.S., and floodlights—but three men, *the author and two others,* achieved the impossible. "A splendid story."—New York *Times.*

These books available at your local newsstand, or send price indicated plus 10¢ per copy for mailing costs to Berkley Publishing Corp., 15 East 26th Street, New York 10, New York.